The Youth Revolution

PROBLEMS IN EUROPEAN CIVILIZATION

Under the editorial direction of
John Ratté
Amherst College

The
Youth Revolution

The Conflict of Generations in Modern History

Edited and with an introduction by

Anthony Esler

College of William and Mary

D. C. HEATH AND COMPANY
Lexington, Massachusetts   Toronto   London

CONTENTS

III GENERATIONAL REVOLT: A FORCE IN HISTORY?

INTRODUCTION

There is probably nothing wholly new under the sun. But history does have its new emphases. A minor matter in one age may emerge as a major force in the next cycle of history. A human potential, dormant through the centuries, may find a favorable environment for development at last, with explosive results for history.

When such "new" trends do surface, new theories usually evolve to explain them. The Industrial Revolution, for instance, put unparalleled economic development squarely in the center of the history of the past two centuries. Not surprisingly, this same astounding economic upsurge gave the economic approach an unprecedentedly high place in the thinking of historians and social scientists.

So it happened also with what is popularly known as the youth revolution of the last century and a half, and with the resulting generational approach to history.

There has always been some conflict between the generations. Aristotle detected a generation gap in ancient Greece. Town-versus-gown battles and apprentice riots were commonplace in the middle ages. Only during the nineteenth and twentieth centuries, however, has a clearly discernible youth revolution become sufficiently important in history to attract the attention of social commentators in general and of historians in particular. And only during the past fifty years has a serious body of generational theory arisen to explain this startling phenomenon.

The widening gap between the generations first became apparent during the restoration period following Napoleon's defeat at Waterloo in 1815. The secret societies which plotted—and sometimes openly revolted—against the restoration of the *ancien régime* were overwhelmingly young, both in membership and in spirit. Groups like the German Student Unions and Mazzini's Young Italy made the youthful barricade fighter and political conspirator one of the accepted counters of European politics. The revolutions of 1848 alone summoned rebellious youth—among other clearly distinguishable groups—into the streets of half the capitals of Europe.

The trend surged on unabated through the second half of the century. Garibaldi's Red Shirts, the bomb-throwing Russian terrorists, and similar groups of young rebels made it clear that the youth revolution was not a temporary wonder. In life, as in literature, the conflict of generations was becoming one of the main themes of modern history.

The first half of the twentieth century saw further developments in the increasingly clamorous revolt of important segments of Europe's youth. The rejection of the established order—social, moral, artistic, and political—by the youth of the post-World War I period was notorious. The emergence of adult-led political youth groups like the Hitler Youth, Mussolini's Sons of the Wolf, or the Russian *Komsomol* were especially notable. These organizations managed to channel successfully the rebellious utopianism of the young into the service of totalitarian revolution.

The decades since World War II have seen an unparalleled growth and spread of youthful political dissidence. The youth revolution has taken many forms in recent years, from the Hungarian and Czech revolts against Russian hegemony to the youthful rebellions of the German SDS or the May Days in Paris that shook Gaullist France to its foundations. Waves of youthful insurgency spread far beyond the shores of Europe—as they had in fact been doing since the early 1900s. These extra-European manifestations of the world-wide youth revolution included such varied instances as the American civil rights and antiwar movements, the stick-wielding Zengakuren in Japan, and the rise of the Red Guard in Communist China. Everywhere, the sign and symbol of the new militance was the same: the overwhelming predominance of young faces, young ideas, young bodies on the line.

These wide-ranging insurrectionary outbursts have taken several basic forms. Youthful secret societies, barricade fighters, and totalitarian youth groups have already been mentioned. Distinctively *student* movements have also played an important part in the youth revolution. So have cadres of young military officers, like the Decembrists in Russia or the Young Turks, and youth-oriented political factions like the Young Czechs.

There have been reformers as well as root-and-branch revolutionaries in the ranks of the young rebels, right-wing as well as left-wing crusaders among them. Some, like the Russian "To the People" movement of the 1870s, have been almost saintly in their commitment to nonviolence. Others, like the terrorists who assassinated the tsar in 1881, have been just as convinced that only violence will change the world. However, all these true believers have one thing in common: youth, and the capacity for total ideological commitment that seems to be peculiar to this tense, impassioned stage of life.

This is the youth revolution of the last century and a half. It is a vast and growing tendency of key segments of the younger generation to revolt against the established order—whatever that order may be. These new rebels share no single ideology, no uniform tactic or single common goal. Their revolt has been sporadic and intermittent, not continuous. As a trend it has been difficult to define. Consequently there are some authorities who reject its very existence, declaring that the generation gap is a pure invention of the journalists or the social scientists.

But the youth revolts of the nineteenth and twentieth centuries have been real—on this at least the case studies that follow are in agreement. The young have been in the streets in unprecedented and growing numbers these past two centuries. To this concrete historical extent, the youth revolution is a reality.

Like the youth revolution, attempts to explain the new militance of the young have taken many forms. Political scientists, sociologists, psychologists, anthropologists, and even philosophers have all tried to define it. So, too, have historians. Almost all these varying approaches, however, have depended to some extent on the notion of the *generation*—the birth cohort or age group—as a force in history.

It is not the individual young malcontent upon whom these interpretations focus, but youth en masse. It is precisely the increasing tendency of sizable sections of an entire birth cohort to adopt heterodox social views, and to act together to implement those views, that makes the rebelliousness of the young historically significant in our time. It is this tendency which makes the youth revolution of concern to the politician and the policeman, the social scientist and the historian. And the simplest and most coherent explanation of the typical youth revolt is to be found in one form or another of the theory of social generations.

The first section of this book, therefore, offers some thoughtful answers to a deceptively simple question: What is a generation in history?

During the nineteenth century, the rhythmic recurrence of revolutionary younger generations seems to have created a new consciousness of the generational process, a consciousness which became increasingly widespread with the accelerating tempo of social change. Sensitive writers and thinkers of all sorts recognized the existence of social generations, speculated about them, or reacted emotionally to their own place in the generational movement of history.

Thinkers as diverse as Goethe, Comte, and John Stuart Mill expressed striking, if scattered and unsystematic, insights into the generational phenomenon. For instance, Goethe revealed his belief that every man's fundamental world view is determined by the experience of his youthful, formative years. Members of the same generation, he suggested, are linked through life by bonds of mutual understanding that set them apart from all others.

Novelists like Flaubert, Tolstoy, Turgenev, and Mann constructed major works of fiction on a framework of generational development and interaction. The fundamental conflict of Turgenev's *Fathers and Sons* (1861), for example, is clearly broader than the single family on which the novel focuses. The clash between the archetypal characters of Uncle Pavel, the man of old-fashioned principle, and the young nihilist Bazarov epitomizes the far-reaching clash between succeeding generations of the Russian intelligentsia as a whole that filled the 1860s with tumult.

Nineteenth-century historians also touched upon the problem of generational conflict from time to time. Ranke, for instance, was not unaware of the potential importance of the generational factor in history. But it was the cultural historian Wilhelm Dilthey who actually began the systematic analysis of the social generation with his essay on the German romantic writer *Novalis* (1865). In this account of Novalis and his generation, particular stress is laid on the importance of specific cultural and social factors which mold the mind of the young. It is with Dilthey that the scholarly theory of social generations has its true beginning.

The fully developed concept, however, did not appear until the twentieth century. The first real burgeoning of serious interest in the generational approach arose some fifty years ago, in the aftermath of World War I.

In 1920, the French scholar François Mentré's doctoral dissertation, *Social Generations,* offered the first real attempt at an analytical history of the idea. Mentré defined a generation in simple terms as "a collective state of mind embodied in a group of human beings, which extends over a period of time comparable to the duration of a genealogical generation." [1] He emphasized generational unity, the mysterious ties that bind members of a single generation together to produce a community of creative activity in many spheres of human endeavor. From the research center to the literary coterie, he declared, the members of a social generation reveal their common outlooks and sometimes even duplicate insights and discoveries.

Mentré's outlook was a casting backwards, a summarizing of the scattered insights of the past. In Spain during the interwar years, the celebrated philosopher and social commentator José Ortega y Gasset made an even greater contribution to the evolving notion of social generations. In such works as *The Modern Theme* (1923) and *Man and Crisis* (1933), he elaborated a basic theory of generations in history.

Ortega believed that each generation passes through a rhythmic evolutionary development of growth, young manhood, gradual rise to power, and eventual domination of society. According to his theory, the period of childhood covers the first fifteen years of life; next comes the period of youth, from ages fifteen to thirty; then the period of initiation into positions of power, from thirty to forty-five; and finally the period of direction and control of society, from forty-five to sixty. For the Spanish philosopher, as for Dilthey earlier, the influences which mold a social generation appear to lie largely in the area of intellectual history. Historic events, for the Spanish thinker, play little part in the shaping of a generation.

Ortega also stresses the significance of the interaction of generations—particularly of the two age groups which participate in the direction of society, as masters and as new initiates, at any given time. When these two generations agree on fundamentals, he asserts, they reinforce each other and impart a sense of harmony and

[1] François Mentré, *Les générations sociales* (Paris, 1920), p. 40.

purpose to their age. When they disagree, the result is an age of polemic and simmering rebellion.

Ortega puts little emphasis on youth, and his narrowly cultural focus and simplistic fifteen-year periods-of-life probably strike most readers as rigid and unconvincing. Nevertheless, the theory of Ortega y Gasset does represent the first fully developed general theory of social generations.

In Germany, meanwhile, the sociologist Karl Mannheim was making a major contribution simply by insisting on the importance of specific sociological influences in the development of a social generation. Mannheim was concerned throughout his career with the world views of classes, sects, and other identifiable subgroups in society—including the social generation. A thorough-going empiricist, however, he always insisted that the social circumstances which shape these group *Weltanschauungen* be clearly delineated. Certainly this is the case with his careful anatomy of the social generation, originally published as a two-part article on "The Problem of Generations" (1928).

The process of social change, Mannheim emphasizes, causes each generation to be different in many ways from its predecessors. In a rapidly changing society, the crucial formative experiences of childhood and youth are bound to be different for each successive generation. The inevitable result is the increasingly radical differences between the generations themselves.

The German sociologist proceeds from this common-sense beginning to a series of subtle but absolutely essential distinctions between the *subgroups* to be found within each social generation. A common birthday, as Mannheim points out, clearly does not guarantee a common life experience. Differences of class, race, religion, and other factors shape a number of differing social types *within* each birth cohort. For instance, urban intellectuals are likely to have little in common with farm boys of the same nominal generation, no matter how closely their birthdays coincide.

Within each of *these* subgroups, furthermore, there is usually to be found not one single monolithic world view, but several. The existence of more than one basic generational response to the pressures of the age has frequently been cited as an objection to the whole generational approach. For Mannheim, such disparity is only sociological common sense. It is in fact these divergent world views

—not a common birth date, nor even exposure to a common sociological environment—which have real historical significance. As we shall see, it is precisely these "generation units," generational contemporaries sharing a *common world view* as well as a common social background, which have made the youth revolution of modern times a reality.

Since World War II, a number of social scientists have read papers and published articles urging their respective disciplines to make greater use of the birth cohort, the social generation, or the political generation as tools of analysis. Of these, political scientist Marvin Rintala's article from the *Encyclopedia of the Social Sciences* is the clearest and most pointed.

Rintala's work is summary rather than seminal in nature. But his explanation of the role of generations in politics is certainly clearer and less weighted with purple prose than Ortega's. It is also considerably less jargon-heavy than Mannheim's. It is reprinted in this book as a lucid account of the generation as the contemporary social scientist is coming to understand the term.

The works of Ortega, Mannheim, and contemporary social scientists like Rintala contain the essence of the generational interpretation of the youth revolution. The various essays in this book offer their own implicit or explicit conceptions of the generation in history, for the notion of social generations is a broad framework for understanding a narrow set of dogmatic theoretical propositions. There is room for a wide range of interpretations under the ample umbrella of the generational approach.

The case studies included in section two of this book represent at least three clearly differing approaches to the phenomenon of generational revolt.

Recognition of the reality of the youth revolution and a generalized consciousness of the growing importance of generational conflict in modern history clearly preceded the formulation of any developed theory of social generations. Among the nineteenth-century historians who sensed the increasingly significant role of rebellious youth as a political force, two are reprinted here: Heinrich von Treitschke and Bolton King.

Heinrich von Treitschke, the ardently nationalistic historian of nineteenth-century Germany, was a product of the same ideological passions that had shaped the insurrectionary *Burschenschaft* (Student Union) generation of 1815. Treitschke's own youth during the 1850s was vitally influenced by militant German nationalists like Friedrich Dahlmann and the aging Ernst Moritz Arndt—the latter one of the idols of the *Burschenschaften* thirty-five years previously. The liberalism of the Student Unions was foreign to Treitschke: disillusioned by the liberal failures of 1848 and 1849, he ended as a firm supporter of Bismarckian autocracy. But his fundamental faith in heroic nationalism and the German cause remained as fierce as any Student Unionist's even in his declining years. This belief clearly infuses the account of the student revolt of 1815—from his *History of Germany in the Nineteenth Century* (1879–94)—included here.

The English reformer Bolton King's scholarly history of the Italian *risorgimento* was widely praised for fairness and balance at the time of its first appearance in the 1890s, and it is still used as a scholarly authority. The author's enthusiastic admiration for Mazzini's brand of idealistic liberal nationalism was evident, however, both in this book and in the *Life of Mazzini* (1902) from which the present selection is taken.

Like the youths who joined Mazzini's secret societies in the 1830s, King revered the famous revolutionary for his exalted moralism and for his indefatigable activism—both qualities which King himself, a leader of the English Idealists deeply involved in slum settlements and educational reform since his Oxford days, deeply shared. Like Treitschke, King displays a special empathy with the youth movement. But where Treitschke emphasizes the rank and file, King focuses on the leadership cadres, the zealots, the totally committed ones who have contributed so much to the modern youth revolution.

Both Treitschke and King offer magisterial—and extremely perceptive—accounts of important nineteenth-century generational revolts. Both these historians, however, offer little more than narrative and descriptive treatments of their own colorful chapters in the ongoing history of the youth revolution. Their narratives are clear and convincing, their descriptions often vivid. But they did operate without benefit of the immense broadening and deepening of historical insight which has resulted from the influence of other social sciences and of psychology upon historians during the present century. Most importantly, these nineteenth-century historians wrote before the theory of social generations itself had taken clear shape. The articles by Lutz, Brower, and Loewanberg, the work of mid-twentieth century scholars, profit considerably from these new historio-graphical developments.

Rolland Ray Lutz's essay on the Viennese Academic Legion during the revolution of 1848 is one of the first studies to build on a foundation of Mannheimian generational theory. It is a pioneering effort, dating as far back as a doctoral dissertation of the 1950s. Lutz, however, does seem to hesitate to go all the way with Mannheim in asserting the objective reality of the social generation as a force in history. While emphasizing the age differences which distinguish radical and liberal wings of the 1848 insurrection in Vienna, Lutz urges us to "guard against literalism and remember that we are dealing with two groups, one of which is only generally younger than the other, but which *think of themselves* as being distinct generations. A generation in this sense," he goes on to assert, "is, after all, only a social myth with only some basis in fact." [2]

This exaggerated generational self-consciousness is an important part of any generational revolt, just as class consciousness is essential for a successful class-based movement. This is not to say that a social generation—or a social class—is *no more than* a social myth, as subsequent readings in this book will make clear.

Daniel R. Brower's study of the backgrounds of radical youth in Russia during the 1840s and 1850s focuses on the social classes from which these rebellious generations sprang. The author's thesis —that these young dissidents did *not* come from the lowest ranks of Russian society—challenges a standard interpretation. The article is of special interest for students of the youth revolution, however, as an exemplary study of this crucial aspect of Mannheimian "location in society"—the influential class backgrounds of the young rebels.

Like Lutz's essay, Brower's goes beyond the sweeping narrative impressionism of Treitschke and King. Like Lutz, Brower turns to specific cases and statistical breakdowns as a means of getting closer to an accurate understanding of the sporadic but persistent rebelliousness of modern youth.

Peter Loewenberg, whose paper on the Nazi generation was originally read before the American Historical Association in 1970,

---

[2] Rolland Ray Lutz, "Fathers and Sons in the Vienna Revolution of 1848," *Journal of Central European Affairs* 22 (July 1962):162.

has a rare double background in history and psychoanalysis. He has made impressive contributions to the recent psychohistorical movement among historians. The present essay clearly reflects this double interest.

Thus, though Loewenberg acknowledges his debt to Karl Mannheim's generationist views, he is more deeply influenced by the psychoanalyst Freud. The result of this mingling of influences, fortunately, is a productive one. Loewenberg's stress on childhood, rather than youth, as crucial to the molding of a social generation is a case in point. This emphasis is psychoanalytically orthodox, but it presents a clear and fruitful challenge to the standard generationist emphasis on *youth,* the stage of life when generational consciousness, cohesion, and militance are greatest. In this and in other matters, the overall result of Loewenberg's probing psychohistorical analysis is to take us closer still to the heart of the youth revolution.

Lutz, Brower, and Loewenberg represent some of the latest scholarly approaches to the modern youth revolt. Their use of statistical, literary, and other evidence beyond the normal purview of the nineteenth-century historian, like their psychological and sociological expertise, has clearly expanded our understanding of the youth revolution as a form of generational conflict.

The last two case studies of generational revolt included here reflect a very different tradition of generational history. As Ortega and others have pointed out, this discovery of the social generation derives in large part from a notable increase in generational *self-*consciousness during the last two centuries. This generational self-awareness has been particularly strong among young people who have found themselves in conflict with the institutions and attitudes of their elders—the generational rebels who are the subject of this book.

Two examples of this generational self-analysis are offered here: a pair of eyewitness descriptions of the Hungarian revolt of 1956 and a radical analysis of the Paris rebellion of 1968.

Mihaly Samson and "Laszlo Beke" were not historians of the youth revolution—they were part of it. They did not have the advantage of a background in generational theory, of psychoanalytic insights, or of statistical evidence. But they did have one special advantage denied to most of the authorities in this book—they were there. They were students in the streets of Budapest when the Hungarian revolt began.

Mihaly Samson, a second-year engineering student at the Technical College of Budapest, was the child of working-class parents in a "workers' state." Yet he joined his fellow students in the emotional late-night rally described in this article, and in the great protest march of the following day. Samson recorded these events within hours of their occurrence in the personal diary which, according to his roommate, he kept with "meticulous, almost obsessive" care.[3]

"Laszlo Beke" is the pseudonym adopted by one of the student leaders of the Budapest uprising. Beke was older than most of the other students at the University of Budapest—twenty-four, a veteran of military service, and married. He had been in minor trouble with the Communist authorities earlier, for taking too much interest in Anglo-American capitalist culture. In 1956, he became one of the organizers of the Students' Revolutionary Council. His first-hand account of the confrontation at the radio station, the first blood shed in the revolution, also comes from the author's journal. Like Samson's report, Beke's has a sense of reality few scholarly analyses can match.

Laszlo Beke fled the country in the wake of the crushing Soviet intervention. He was living in exile in Canada at the time he wrote his book. Mihaly Samson was not so fortunate. He was shot through the head in front of the radio station the day after he wrote the diary entry reprinted in this book.

The husband and wife team of Barbara and John Ehrenreich, who have written on such issues as health care abuses, working conditions, and feminism, have been among the most consistent and indefatigable younger critics of our society. Like Samson and Beke, the Ehrenreichs were still students when they wrote their book on the youth revolt of the 1960s. Like the two Hungarian freedom fighters, they were part of the massive generational upheaval which they describe.

The Ehrenreichs were active in the American student movement

[3] Quoted from a letter by Samson's (unidentified) roommate in Tibor Meray, *That Day in Budapest: October 23, 1956,* translated by Charles Lam Markmann (New York, 1969), p. 18.

of the later 1960s. When they set out to study European student militance first-hand, they found plenty of radical friends to introduce them around. On the basis of the resulting interviews in England, France, Germany, Italy—and at the Columbia occupation in New York—they wrote *Long March, Short Spring* (1969), the fact-packed volume of reportage and analysis from which the selection reprinted in this book is taken.

The special value of the Ehrenreichs' work seems to lie in their straightforward emphasis on the issues—the actual demands and ideological orientations of the student rebels themselves—for the youth revolution has never been reducible to simple historical narrative, to social origins or psychological drives, nor even to the contagious momentum of street action. The youth revolution has claimed to be built on ideas and ideals. The Ehrenreichs take these ideological commitments seriously. Their account of the fantastic May Days in Paris enables the reader to do so too.

The first selections reproduced in this book embody some of the major attempts to define a "generation" in history. Subsequent readings examine some of the suggested sources of the youth revolution through case studies of major youth revolts of the last two centuries. The book concludes with an aspect of the problem of generations perhaps even more important than the nature and origins of the movement—its significance in modern history.

Does any of this really *matter,* after all, in the tangled web that is the history of our times? Are the periodic outbursts that comprise the youth revolution really worthy of any particular notice, historically speaking? Or is the conflict of generations really no more than a colorful sideshow, an occasional distraction from the main current of modern history?

Both the scholarly community and the general public have tended to disagree among themselves on the matter.

Popular recognition of the generation as a social unit and popular belief in the growing importance of the younger generation have been widespread at least since the turn of the twentieth century. Since before World War I, journalists and popular pundits have been interviewing young people, compiling compendia of youthful opinion, and generally heaping attention and praise on today's youth. Philippe Ariès, in his widely read *Centuries of Childhood,* goes so far as to label ours "the century of adolescence." In the twentieth century, he declares, "youth . . . became a literary theme and a subject of concern for moralists and politicians. People began wondering seriously what youth was thinking. . . . Youth gave the impression of secretly possessing new values capable of reviving an aged and sclerosed society."[4]

Not everyone, however, has agreed with this assertion of the awesome potential of each new younger generation. The memoirs-of-my-own-generation type of autobiography, which has flourished in this century, provides plenty of evidence of negative judgments on ideologically motivated youth in revolt. Looking back on her own youth, on the role her generation had tried—and failed—to play in history, Margaret McCarthy, a reformed radical of the 1930s, wondered

> *how it had become possible that we, the babies of the First World War, the urchins of the depression, the survivors of the terrors and devastations of World War II—that we, who knew all the answers, in our turn should be leaving our problems unsolved and passing on to our children our own awful heritage of hatred, conflict, and bloodshed.*[5]

Rebellious younger generations repeatedly announced their intention of saving the world. Many people doubted it—including some of these same young people in their later years.

The response of modern scholars to the widening generation gap has been at least as varied as the layman's. Newspaper readers from the Germany of 1815 to the America of 1970 have found the youth revolution intriguing, irritating, laughable, inspiring, and horrifying, according to their own inclinations and the shifting twists and turns of the youth revolts themselves. So, too, scholars—historians among them—have alternately eulogized and damned rebellious youth. They have admired the young rebels, analyzed them, criticized them. They have shrugged off the youth revolution as beneath contempt—or they have discovered in it an almost millennial potential for the building of a brave new world.

The readings reprinted in the third section of this book illustrate this range of reactions. All have been chosen from the most recent spate of scholarly comment on the generation gap, though they

---

[4] Philippe Ariès, *Centuries of Childhood,* trans. Robert Baldick (London, 1962), p. 30.
[5] Margaret McCarthy, *Generation in Revolt* (London, 1953), p. v.

typically draw upon nineteenth- as well as twentieth-century examples to support their arguments.

Perhaps the most widely discussed historical treatment of the youth revolution as a whole to come out of the great explosion of youthful dissent of the 1960s was not by a historian at all. It is Lewis Feuer's *The Conflict of Generations* (1969), the weighty, psychologically, and sociologically informed volume whose introductory pages are included here.

Feuer was himself involved in student politics in the 1930s; hence, he might be expected to offer a strongly positive evaluation of the revolt of the young. In the 1960s, however, he was teaching at the University of California at Berkeley when the Free Speech Movement erupted there—the first great campus upheaval of the turbulent sixties. Perhaps influenced by this experience on the receiving end of a youth revolt, Feuer offers an essentially negative view of the role of revolutionary youth in history. For all their idealism, he says, the young dissenters not only have failed to build a brave new world, but also have frequently left the world worse off than when they took to the streets.

Herbert Moller's approach to the problem of generational revolt in history is that of the demographer, the student of population trends. The article reprinted in this book reflects the author's belief that the youth revolution of modern times is primarily a consequence of demographic changes—particularly of the rapid growth in sheer numbers of young people in this age of exploding populations. He focuses not on the causes, but on the historic significance of this unprecedented upsurge of ideologically impelled youth movements. Here Moller, like Feuer, reveals himself as no enthusiast for the young rebels and their sometimes violent crusades. Unlike Feuer, however, Moller does seem to feel that rebellious youth may have considerable historic potential as a force for social change.

Anthony Esler's contribution, finally, offers an even more positive summing up of the historic significance of the youth revolution. Like Samson, Beke and the Ehrenreichs, Esler has been influenced by his modest participation in protest marches, street demonstrations, and the like. Like Treitschke and King, he has shared many of the convictions of the ongoing youth revolution. Like Moller and Feuer, however, he has come to recognize the distinct weaknesses of youth movements as manipulators of history. Youth will not save the world tomorrow—probably not even the day after. Nevertheless, Esler's article expresses a continuing belief in the immense *long-range* power of generational revolt as a real, if uncontrolled and ill-understood, force for change. This 1972 paper on the historic consequences of a youth rebellion of a century and a half ago goes so far as to suggest that, in a world of accelerating social change and an ever-widening generation gap, the conflict of generations may emerge as one of the most powerful social forces of our times.

Conflict of Opinion

The generation is a dynamic compromise between mass and individual, and it is the most important conception in history.

JOSÉ ORTEGA Y GASSET

The problem of generations is important enough to merit serious consideration. It is one of the indispensable guides to an understanding of the structure of social and intellectual movements.

KARL MANNHEIM

This is a book about the workings of the ethical, idealistic spirit in human history. For of all social movements, those composed of students have been characterized by the highest degree of selflessness, generosity, compassion, and readiness for self-sacrifice. And this is also a book about how the idealistic spirit has done violence to itself and to others, and has been transmuted into a destructive force in human history.

LEWIS S. FEUER

[The leaders of the German Student Unions] regarded themselves as lords of this small academic realm, all the more because most of the professors exhibited for these youthful tyrants a quite immoderate veneration, compounded of fear and benevolence; even now, the leaders of the *Burschenschaft* looked forward to the time when their organization would rule all Germany.

HENRICH VON TREITSCHKE

Mazzini had at this time a supreme faith in his generation . . . "this young Italy of ours," so vigorous and cultured and warmhearted, that no new movement, however bold and difficult, was beyond its powers. "Place," he said now, "the young at the head of the insurgent masses; you do not know what strength is latent in these young hands, what magic influence the voice of the young has on the crowd; you will find in them a host of apostles for the new religion."

BOLTON KING

We must, then, guard against literalism and remember that we are dealing with two groups, one of which is only generally younger than the other, but which think of themselves as being distinct generations. A "generation" in this sense is, after all, a social myth with only some basis in fact.

ROLLAND RAY LUTZ

Still, the "father-son" argument which Turgenev initiated in his novel may have more meaning for the origins of the radical intellectuals than realized until now. . . . Somehow, somewhere in the upbringing of this small group of rebels, there occurred a fundamental rupture with the beliefs and outlook accepted by their family, their class, their society.

DANIEL R. BROWER

The war and postwar experiences of the small children and youth of World War I explicitly conditioned the nature and success of National Socialism. The new adults who became politically effective after 1929 and who filled the ranks of the SA and other paramilitary party organizations such as the Hitler-Jugend and the Bund-Deutscher-Mädel were the children socialized in the First World War.

PETER LOEWENBERG

Then the forty-five-year-old police major stepped up toward us and saluted me, a young man of twenty-five. "All right, boys," he said with a weak smile. . . . He stood back with other police as we piled tommy-guns, automatic weapons, hand grenades, and other arms on two trucks parked in the yard.

LASZLO BEKE

Back in June, a March 22nd activist told us that the students might not be able to carry through the revolution, might even become counter-revolutionary. "But it doesn't matter," he continued, "because the six-teen-year-olds, the thirteen-year-olds, are revolutionary now. They will push us out of the way and go on by themselves someday."

BARBARA AND JOHN EHRENREICH

The presence of a large contingent of young people in a population may make for a cumulative process of innovation and social and cultural growth; it may lead to elemental, directionless acting-out behavior; it may destroy old institutions and elevate new elites to power; and the unemployed energies of the young may be organized and directed by totalitarian rulers. The dynamism of its large and youthful populations distinguishes the crowded history of the twentieth century.

HERBERT MOLLER

I   WHAT IS A GENERATION?

José Ortega y Gasset

THE IMPORTANCE OF GENERATIONHOOD

José Ortega y Gasset (1883–1955), the Spanish philosopher, wrote, taught, and lectured on a wide variety of subjects—political, social, historical and philosophical. Though he studied at distinguished Spanish and German universities and was for twenty-five years professor of metaphysics at the University of Madrid, most of Ortega's writings originally appeared in magazines and in newspapers.

The extracts which follow first appeared in book form in The Modern Theme (El tema de nuestro tiempo, *1923) and in* Man and Crisis (En torno a Galileo, *1933). The first selection is the author's initial formal presentation of the generational approach to history; the second is from his most thorough analysis of the subject. In these passages, Ortega's conviction that the rhythmic succession of generations plays a crucial role in social change finds eloquent expression.*

The changes in vital sensibility which are decisive in history, appear under the form of the generation. A generation is not a handful of outstanding men, nor simply a mass of men; it resembles a new integration of the social body, with its select minority and its gross multitude, launched upon the orbit of existence with a pre-established vital trajectory. The generation is a dynamic compromise between mass and individual, and is the most important conception in history. It is, so to speak, the pivot responsible for the movements of historical evolution.

A generation is a variety of the human race in the strict sense given to that term by naturalists. Its members come into the world endowed with certain typical characteristics which lend them a common physiognomy, distinguishing them from the previous generation. Beneath this general sign of identity, individuals of so diverse a temper can exist that, being compelled to live in close contact with one another, inasmuch as they are contemporaries, they often find themselves mutually antipathetic. But under the most violent oppo-

From José Ortega y Gasset, *The Modern Theme,* translated by James Cleugh (New York: Harper and Row, 1961), pp. 14–15, 16–18; also reprinted from *Man and Crisis* by José Ortega y Gasset. Translated from the Spanish by Mildred Adams. By permission of W. W. Norton and Company, Inc. Copyright © 1958 by W. W. Norton and Company, Inc., pp. 40–41, 44–45, and by permission of George Allen and Unwin Ltd., London.

sition of "pros" and "antis" it is easy to perceive a real union of interests. Both parties consist of men of their own time; and great as their differences may be their mutual resemblances are still greater. The reactionary and the revolutionary of the nineteenth century are much nearer to one another than either is to any man of our own age. The fact is, that whether they are black or white the men of that generation belong to one species, while in our own persons, whether we are black or white, are the beginnings of a further and distinct variety of mankind. . . .

Life . . . for each generation is a task in two dimensions, one of which consists in the reception, through the agency of the previous generation, of what has had life already, e.g., ideas, values, institutions and so on, while the other is the liberation of the creative genius inherent in the generation concerned. The attitude of the generation cannot be the same towards its own active agency as towards what it has received from without. What has been done by others, that is, executed and perfected in the sense of being completed, reaches us with a peculiar unction attached to it: it seems consecrated, and in view of the fact that we have not ourselves assisted in its construction, we tend to believe that it is the work of no one in particular, even that it is reality itself. There is a moment at which the concepts of our teachers do not appear to us to be the opinions of particular men, but truth itself come to dwell anonymously upon the earth. On the other hand our spontaneous sensibility, the thoughts and feelings which are our private possessions, never seem to us properly finished, complete and fixed, like a definite object: we regard them more as a species of internal flux, composed of less stable elements. This disadvantage is compensated by the greater expansiveness and adaptability to our own nature always characteristic of spontaneity.

The spirit of every generation depends upon the equation established between these two ingredients and on the attitude which the majority of the individuals concerned adopts towards each. Will that majority surrender to its inheritance, ignoring the internal promptings of spontaneity? Or will it obey the latter and defy the authority of the past? There have been generations which felt that there was a perfect similarity between their inheritance and their own private possessions. The consequence, then, is that ages of accumulation arise. Other times have felt a profound dissimilarity between the two factors, and then there ensue ages of elimination and dispute, generations in conflict. In the former case the young men coming to the front coalesce with the old and submit to them: in politics, in science and in the arts the ancient *régime* continues. Such periods belong to the old. In the latter case, since there is no attempt at preservation and accumulation, but on the contrary a movement towards relegation and substitution, the old are swept away by youth. Such periods belong to the young and are years of innovation and creative struggle. . . .

            *   *   *

Until he is twenty-five years old, man normally does little but learn, receive information about the things that make up his social environment—his teachers, the books, the conversations that surround him. In those years he becomes aware of what the world is, he comes up against the aspects of a world which he finds already made. . . . The young man finds himself caught in this world at twenty-five, and throws himself into living in it on his own account, that is to say, he too takes his place in the world making. But as he meditates on the world in force (the world of the men who in his time are mature) his thesis, his problems, his doubts, are very different from those which these mature men felt when in their own youth they in turn meditated on the world of those who were then mature (men who are now very old), and so on backwards.

If we are considering only one or two young men who react to the world of the mature, the modifications to which their meditations will lead them will be very few, possibly important at some point, but in the last analysis only partial. One could not say that their activity changes the world.

But this is not a matter of just a few young men; it touches all those who are young at a certain date, who are rather more in number than the ones who are mature. Each youth will be particularly active at one point of the horizon; but between them they will bring pressure to bear on the entire horizon,—some of them on art, others on religion or one of the sciences, on industry, on politics. The modifications which they produce at each point have to be minimal; yet we must recognize that they have changed the whole face of the world so that years later, when another crowd of youngsters start their life, they will find themselves with a world looking entirely different from what it did when their elders met it. . . .

Community of date and of space are . . . the primary attributes of a generation. Together they signify the sharing of an essential destiny. The keyboard of environment on which coevals must play the *sonata apassionata* of their lives is in its fundamental structure one and the same. This identity of destiny produces in coevals certain secondary coincidences which are summed up in the unity of their vital style.

At one time I pictured a generation as "a caravan within which man moves a prisoner, but at the same time, a voluntary one at heart, and content. He moves within it faithful to the poets of his age, to the political ideas of his time, to the type of woman triumphant in his youth, and even to the fashion of walking which he employed at twenty-five. From time to time he sees another caravan pass with a strange and curious profile; this is the other generation. Perhaps celebrations on a feast day may bring the two together, may blend them; but as the hour of normal living approaches the somewhat chaotic fusion divides into two organic groups. Each individual mysteriously recognizes all of the rest of his collectivity, as the ants in each ant hill recognize each other by a peculiar pattern of odor.

"The discovery that we are fatally inscribed within a certain group having its own age and style of life is one of the melancholy experiences which, sooner or later, befalls every sensitive man. A generation is an integrated manner of existence, or, if you prefer, a fashion in living, which fixes itself indelibly on the individual. Among certain savage peoples the members of each coeval group are recognized by their tattooing. The fashion in epidermal design which was in vogue when they were adolescents has remained encrusted in their beings."

In the "today," in every "today," various generations coexist and the relations which are established between them, according to the different condition of their ages, represent the dynamic system of attractions and repulsions, of agreement and controversy, which at any given moment makes up the reality of historic life. The concept of the generations, converted into a method of historic investigation, consists in nothing more than projecting that structure across the past. Everything else is a refusal to discover the authentic reality of human life at a given time, a renouncing of the mission of history. . . .

Karl Mannheim

WHAT IS A SOCIAL GENERATION?

Karl Mannheim (1893–1947), the German sociologist, was educated in Germany and taught primarily at Heidelberg until the Nazis came to power in 1933. Thereafter, he taught at the London School of Economics until his death. Mannheim's major works include Ideology and Utopia *(1929) and* Man and Society in an Age of Reconstruction *(1935).*

Mannheim was concerned throughout his scholarly life with the differing world views of ages, classes, and other subgroups in society. The present essay, which first appeared in the Kölner Vierteljahrshefte für Soziologie *in 1928 as a two-part study of "The Problem of Generations," seeks to get at the sociological roots of the ties that bind a social generation.*

This, then, broadly constitutes those aspects of generation phenomena which can be deduced by formal analysis. They would completely determine the effects resulting from the existence of generations if they could unfold themselves in a purely biological context, or if the generation phenomenon could be understood as a mere location phenomenon. However, a generation in the sense of a location phenomenon falls short of encompassing the generation phenomenon in its full actuality. The latter is something more than the former, in the same way as the mere fact of class position does not yet involve the existence of a consciously constituted class. The location as such only contains potentialities which may materialize, or be suppressed, or become embedded in other social forces and manifest themselves in modified form. When we pointed out that mere coexistence in time did not even suffice to bring about community of generation location, we came very near to making the distinction which is now claiming our attention. In order to share the same generation location, i.e. in order to be able passively to undergo or actively to use the handicaps and privileges inherent in a generation location, one must be born within the same historical and cultural region. Generation as an actuality, however, involves

From *Essays on the Sociology of Knowledge*, by Karl Mannheim, edited by Paul Kecskemeti (Oxford University Press, 1952), pp. 302–310. Reprinted by permission. Also by permission of Routledge and Kegan Paul, Ltd., London. Footnotes omitted.

even more than mere co-presence in such a historical and social region. A further concrete nexus is needed to constitute generation as an actuality. This additional nexus may be described as *participation in the common destiny* of this historical and social unit. This is the phenomenon we have to examine next.

We said above that, for example, young people in Prussia about 1800 did not share a common generation location with young people in China at the same period. Membership in the same historical community, then, is the widest criterion of community of generation location. But what is its narrowest criterion? Do we put the peasants, scattered as they are in remote districts and almost untouched by current upheavals, in a common actual generation group with the urban youth of the same period? Certainly not!—and precisely because they remain unaffected by the events which move the youth of the towns. We shall therefore speak of a *generation as an actuality* only where a concrete bond is created between members of a generation by their being exposed to the social and intellectual symptoms of a process of dynamic destabilization. Thus, the young peasants we mentioned above only share the same generation location, without, however, being members of the same generation as an actuality, with the youth of the town. They are similarly located, in so far as they are *potentially* capable of being sucked into the vortex of social change, and, in fact, this is what happened in the wars against Napoleon, which stirred up all German classes. For these peasants' sons, a mere generation location was transformed into membership of a generation as an actuality. Individuals of the same age, they were and are, however, only united as an actual generation in so far as they participate in the characteristic social and intellectual currents of their society and period, and in so far as they have an active or passive experience of the interactions of forces which made up the new situation. At the time of the wars against Napoleon, nearly all social strata were engaged in such a process of give and take, first in a wave of war enthusiasm, and later in a movement of religious revivalism. Here, however, a new question arises. Suppose we disregard all groups which do *not* actively participate in the process of social transformation—does this mean that all those groups which *do* so participate, constitute one generation? From 1800 on, for instance, we see two contrasting groups—one which became more and more conservative as time went on, as against a youth group tending to become rationalistic and liberal. It cannot be said that these two groups were unified by the *same* modern mentality. Can we then speak, in this case, of the same actual generation? We can, it seems, if we make a further terminological distinction. Both the romantic-conservative and the liberal-rationalist youth belonged to the same actual generation, romantic-conservatism and liberal-rationalism were merely two *polar forms* of the intellectual and social response to an historical stimulus experienced by all in common. Romantic-conservative youth, and liberal-rationalist group, belong to the same actual generation but form separate "generation units" within it. The *generation unit* represents a much more concrete bond than the actual generation as such. *Youth experiencing the same concrete historical problems may be said to be part of the same actual generation; while those groups within the same actual generation which work up the material of their common experiences in different specific ways, constitute separate generation units.*

The question now arises, what produces a generation unit? In what does the greater intensity of the bond consist in this case? The first thing that strikes one on considering any particular generation unit is the great similarity in the data making up the consciousness of its members. Mental data are of sociological importance not only because of their actual content, but also because they cause the individuals sharing them to form one group—they have a socializing effect. The concept of Freedom, for example, was important for the liberal generation-unit, not merely because of the material demands implied by it, but also because in and through it it was possible to unite individuals scattered spatially and otherwise. The data as such, however, are not the primary factor producing a group—this function belongs to a far greater extent to those formative forces which shape the data and give them character and direction. From the casual slogan to a reasoned system of thought, from the apparently isolated gesture to the finished work of art, the same formative tendency is often at work—the social importance of which lies in its power to bind individuals socially together. The profound emotional significance of a slogan, of an expressive gesture, or of a work of art lies in the fact that we not merely absorb them as objective data, but also as vehicles of formative tendencies and fundamental integrative attitudes, thus identifying ourselves with a set of collective strivings.

Fundamental integrative attitudes and formative principles are all-important also in the handing down of every tradition, firstly because they alone can bind groups together, secondly, and, what is perhaps even more important, they alone are really capable of becoming the basis of continuing practice. A mere statement of fact has a minimum capacity of initiating a continuing practice. Potentialities of a continued thought process, on the other hand, are contained in every thesis that has real group-forming potency; intuitions, feelings, and works of art which create a spiritual community among men also contain in themselves the potentially new manner in which the intuition, feeling, or work of art in question can be re-created, rejuvenated and reinterpreted in novel situations. That is why unambiguousness, too great clarity is not an unqualified social value; productive misunderstanding is often a condition of continuing life. Fundamental integrative attitudes and formative principles are the primary socializing forces in the history of society, and it is necessary to live them fully in order really to participate in collective life.

Modern psychology provides more and more conclusive evidence in favor of the Gestalt theory of human perception: even in our most elementary perceptions of objects, we do not behave as the old atomistic psychology would have us believe; that is, we do not proceed towards a global impression by the gradual summation of a number of elementary sense data, but on the contrary, we start off with a global impression of the object as a whole. Now if even sense perception is governed by the Gestalt principle, the same applies, to an even greater extent, to the process of intellectual interpretation. There may be a number of reasons why the functioning of human consciousness should be based on the Gestalt principle, but a likely factor is the relatively limited capacity of the human consciousness when confronted with the infinity of elementary data which can be dealt with only by means of the simplifying and summarizing Gestalt approach. Seeing things in terms of Gestalt, however, also has its social roots with which we must deal here. Perceptions and their linguistic expressions never exist exclusively for the isolated individual who happens to entertain them, but also for the social group which stands behind the individual. Thus, the way in which seeing in terms of Gestalt modifies the datum as such—partly simplifying and abbreviating it, partly elaborating and filling it out—always corresponds to the meaning which the object in question has for the social groups as a whole. We always see things already formed in a special way; we think concepts defined in terms of a specific context. Form and context depend, in any case, on the group to which we belong. To become really assimilated into a group involves more than the mere acceptance of its characteristic values —it involves the ability to see things from its particular "aspect," to endow concepts with its particular shade of meaning, and to experience psychological and intellectual impulses in the configuration characteristic of the group. It means, further, to absorb those interpretive formative principles which enable the individual to deal with new impressions and events in a fashion broadly predetermined by the group.

The social importance of these formative and interpretive principles is that they form a link between spatially separated individuals who may never come into personal contact at all. Whereas mere common "location" in a generation is of only potential significance, a generation as an actuality is constituted when similarly "located" contemporaries participate in a common destiny and in the ideas and concepts which are in some way bound up with its unfolding. Within this community of people with a common destiny there can then arise particular *generation-units.* These are characterized by the fact that they do not merely involve a loose participation by a number of individuals in a pattern of events shared by all alike though interpreted by the different individuals differently, but an identity of responses, a certain affinity in the way in which all move with and are formed by their common experiences.

Thus within any generation there can exist a number of differentiated, antagonistic generation-units. Together they constitute an "actual" generation precisely because they are oriented toward each other, even though only in the sense of fighting one another. Those who were young about 1810 in Germany constituted one actual generation whether they adhered to the then current version of liberal or conservative ideas. But in so far as they were conservative or liberal, they belonged to different units of that actual generation.

The generation-unit tends to impose a much more concrete and binding tie on its members because of the parallelism of responses it involves. As a matter of fact, such new, overtly created, partisan integrative attitudes characterizing generation-units do not come into being spontaneously, without a personal contact among individuals, but within *concrete groups* where mutual stimulation in a close-knit vital unit inflames the participants and enables them to develop integrative attitudes which do justice to the requirements inherent in their common "location." Once developed in this way, however, these attitudes and formative tendencies are capable of being detached from the concrete groups of their origin and of exercising an appeal and binding force over a much wider area.

The generation-unit as we have described it is not, as such, a concrete group, although it does have as its nucleus a concrete group which has developed the most essential new conceptions which are subsequently developed by the unit. Thus, for example, the set of basic ideas which became prevalent in the development of modern German Conservatism had its origin in the concrete association *"Christlich-deutsche Tischgesellschaft."* This association was first to take up and deformulate all the irrational tendencies corresponding to the overall situation prevailing at that time, and to the particular "location," in terms of generation, shared by the young Conservatives. Ideas which later were to have recruiting power in far wider circles originated in this particular concrete group.

The reason for the influence exercised beyond the limits of the original concrete group by such integrative attitudes originally evolved within the group is primarily that they provide a more or less adequate expression of the particular "location" of a generation as a whole. Hence, individuals outside the narrow group but nevertheless similarly located find in them the satisfying expression of their location in the prevailing *historical configuration.* Class ideology, for example, originates in more closely knit concrete groups and can gain ground only to the extent that other individuals see in it a more or less adequate expression and interpretation of the experiences peculiar to their particular *social* location. Similarly, the basic integrative attitudes and formative principles represented by a generation-unit, which are originally evolved within such a concrete group, are only really effective and capable of expansion into wider spheres when they formulate the typical experiences of the individuals sharing a generation location. Concrete groups can become influential in this sense if they succeed in evolving a "fresh contact" in terms of a "stratification of experience," such as we have described above. There is, in this respect, a further analogy between the phenomenon of class and that of generation. Just as a class ideology may, in epochs favorable to it, exercise an appeal beyond the "location" which is its proper habitat, certain impulses particular to a generation may, if the trend of the times is favorable to them, also attract individual members of earlier or later age groups.

But this is not all; it occurs very frequently that the nucleus of attitudes particular to a new generation is first evolved and practiced by older people who are isolated in their own generation (fore-runners), just as it is often the case that the forerunners in the development of a particular class ideology belong to a quite alien class.

All this, however, does not invalidate our thesis that there are new basic impulses attributable to a particular generation location which, then, may call forth generation units. The main thing in this respect is that the proper vehicle of these new impulses is always a collectivity. The real seat of the class ideology remains the class itself, with its own typical opportunities and handicaps—even when the author of the ideology, as it may happen, belongs to a different class, or when the ideology expands and becomes influential beyond the limits of the class location. Similarly, the real seat of new impulses remains the generation location (which will selectively encourage one form of experience and eliminate others), even when they may have been fostered by other age groups.

The most important point we have to notice is the following: not every generation location—not even every age group—creates new collective impulses and formative principles original to itself and adequate to its particular situation. Where this does happen, we shall speak of a *realization of potentialities inherent* in the location, and it appears probable that the frequency of such realizations is closely connected with the tempo of social change. When as a result of an acceleration in the tempo of social and cultural transformation basic attitudes must change so quickly that the latent, continuous adaptation and modification of traditional patterns of experience, thought, and expression is no longer possible, then the various new phases of experience are consolidated somewhere, forming a clearly distinguishable new impulse, and a new center of configuration. We speak in such cases of the formation of a new generation style, or of a new *generation entelechy.*

Here too, we may distinguish two possibilities. On the one hand, the generation unit may produce its work and deeds unconsciously out of the new impulse evolved by itself, having an intuitive awareness of its existence as a group but failing to realize the group's character as a generation unit. On the other hand, groups may consciously experience and emphasize their character as generation units—as is the case with the contemporary German youth movement, or even to a certain extent with its forerunner, the Student's Association (*Burschenschaft*) Movement in the first half of the nineteenth century, which already manifested many of the characteristics of the modern youth movement.

The importance of the acceleration of social change for the realization of the potentialities inherent in a generation location is clearly demonstrated by the fact that largely static or very slowly changing communities like the peasantry display no such phenomenon as new generation units sharply set off from their predecessors by virtue of an individual entelechy proper to them; in such communities, the tempo of change is so gradual that new generations evolve away from their predecessors without any visible break, and all we can see is the purely biological differentiation and affinity based upon difference or identity of age. Such biological factors are effective, of course, in modern society too, youth being attracted to youth and age to age. The generation unit as we have described it, however, could not arise solely on the basis of this simple factor of attraction between members of the same age group.

The quicker the tempo of social and cultural change is, then, the greater are the chances that particular generation location groups will react to changed situations by producing their own entelechy. . . .

Marvin Rintala

GENERATIONS IN POLITICS

Marvin Rintala (b.1934) is a professor of political science at Boston College. His special field of interest lies in twentieth-century Finnish political movements, but his interest in the generational approach transcends this particular application of it. His works include Three Generations: The Extreme Right Wing in Finnish Politics *(1962) and* Essays on Generational Themes *(1974).*

The present article, from the International Encyclopedia of the Social Sciences *(second edition, 1968), offers a lucid summary of the development and conflict of generations as a factor in the political life of modern times—the fundamental theme of all the essays to follow.*

Group consciousness is universally recognized as one of the fundamental elements of political motivation. Individual human beings in every political system seek the security provided by membership in groups. Group consciousness is created by certain basic similarities, and this consciousness in turn creates more homogeneity within the group, a conformity which often leads to common action. Individuals think of themselves as members of a group and therefore act as members of that group. Since the interests of different groups are not always mutually compatible, there is social conflict. Since all individuals have allegiances to more than one group, there is conflict within the individual, who must decide which group is most important to him in given circumstances. In European politics, for instance, there has often been a conflict between national consciousness and class consciousness, which has generally been resolved in favor of the former.

Although political scientists have studied intensively both national consciousness and class consciousness, they have not explored to any considerable extent another kind of group consciousness, that of belonging to a distinct generation. This omission is surprising, for novelists, cultural and political historians, and sociologists have all used the concept of generation with considerable success. Although **Turgenev's** *Fathers and Sons* is the outstanding example of a literary work in which different generations cannot communicate effectively with each other, generational conflict is one of the major themes running through most of world literature. This fact is perhaps responsible for the emphasis which cultural historians have given to the study of different literary, artistic, and musical generations. Sometimes, indeed, cultural historians have seen only the successive alternation of "romantic" and "classical" generations. Historians, among them Ranke, have speculated about the significance of a generations approach to political history. Sociologists, especially Karl Mannheim (1928) and Rudolf Heberle (1951), have emphasized the importance of generational differences in social movements and social change. Political scientists, however, have used political generation as a conceptual tool only in the study of modern totalitarianism. Sigmund Neumann (1939; 1942) convincingly stressed the generational consciousness of National Socialist leaders and followers. Students of Soviet politics have found basic differences, not attributable merely to life cycle differences, between the responses of younger and older generations to the enforcement of conformity within the Soviet Union.

It could be argued that the concept of political generation can be of major assistance in understanding the motivation of leaders and followers in all political systems, not merely those which are totalitarian. Much of the hesitance of political scientists in applying this concept undoubtedly has arisen from uncertainty as to the precise meaning of a generation in politics. A political generation is not to be equated with a biological generation. Political generations do not suddenly "change" every thirty or thirty-five years. The process of social change is continuous, and it cannot wait until political power is handed on from father to son. There is undoubtedly much personal conflict between fathers and sons, but most of this conflict has no direct political significance. The history of politics is not primarily that of conflict, or even of consensus, between fathers and sons—although such conflict may take place, as it did between James and John Stuart Mill, with important political consequences. There are always—assuming a minimal rate of social change—more than two generations in politics at any one time. The idea of a "young" generation and an "old" generation as the sole participants in the political process is as oversimplified as Karl Marx's assumption that there are only two classes in modern industrial society. The idea of two

generations in politics is frequently linked with the erroneous assumption that the "young" generation is always liberal and the "old"
generation is always conservative.

Implicit in a generations approach to politics is the assumption
that an individual's political attitudes do not undergo substantial
change during the course of his adult lifetime. Once a set of political
beliefs has been embraced, it is regarded as unlikely that the individual will abandon his beliefs. Rather than altering his previous
outlook on the basis of new facts, the individual either rejects or
accepts these new facts depending on whether or not they are consistent with his previous outlook. In this sense, a "liberal" generation
will remain "liberal" in terms of the formative years throughout the
physical lifetime of its members. Whether this same political attitude
will appear liberal under radically changed circumstances is another
matter. Much of the confusion in the political vocabulary of any
nation may be due to the different meanings given to the same term
by members of different generations. In thus explaining the tenacity
of "outmoded" policies, generations theory removes these policies
from the realm of free choice, from the realm of moral judgments.
In this respect, a generations approach has the same fundamental
weaknesses and strengths as any other determinist approach.

Especially in times of rapid social change, it is important to know
precisely at what period of life political attitudes are formed. It is interesting that no serious advocate of a generations approach has
argued that political attitudes are formed during childhood. Rather,
it is argued that late adolescence and early adulthood are the formative years during which a distinctive personal outlook on politics
emerges, which remains essentially unchanged through old age. The
crucial years are regarded as approximately seventeen to twenty-five.
If these years are in fact formative, neither the years preceding nor
the years following them are decisive in the formation of political
attitudes. It is during the formative years that the youth discovers
his own identity. When he defines who he is in terms of society, he
defines his political outlook as well. A political generation is seen
as a group of individuals who have undergone the same basic historical experiences during their formative years. Such a generation
would find political communication with earlier and later generations
difficult, if not impossible.

. . . Not all historical events are experienced to the same degree by the same number of individuals in their formative years, and political generations therefore vary widely in size. The 1825 Decembrist conspiracy, for instance, decisively influenced a much smaller number of young Russians than did the Russian revolution of 1917. Assuming that the total degree of political participation is stable, it is the temporal and spatial "limits" of a given historic event that define the size of the resulting political generation, just as the degree of uniqueness of that event determines the degree of difficulty that generation will have in communicating with earlier and later generations. In this sense, for instance, the political generation created by World War I was a general European phenomenon. It was neither worldwide nor confined to one or a few European nations. The enormous transformation of European society which the war involved meant that a new political generation was created throughout Europe. But the limited nature of the war experience outside Europe meant that the war had far less impact on, say, American or Japanese youth. Those Europeans whose formative years, in whole or in part, occurred during 1914–1918, especially those who actually fought in the war, were not all influenced in the same way; but they were nevertheless all decisively influenced by it. Their reactions to the war were often very different, depending upon their national, class, and especially, personality differences. In a real sense, the fact that they were all involved in the war in their formative years determined their attitude toward politics for the rest of their lives. Some never recovered from the war and retreated from politics, which had, they felt, led directly to such suffering. Others entered politics after 1918 determined above all to prevent a recurrence of war. Still others never spiritually left the battlefield and as a result engaged in politics as the continuation of war by other means. These three alternatives formed what Karl Mannheim termed "generation units," which together constituted a generation precisely because they were oriented toward one another, if only to fight one another. Politics involves more than knowledge of friend and foe, but many of the personal friendships and enmities which in fact later influence political behavior originate during the formative years. Each generation speaks out with more than one voice—there is conflict within each generation as well as among generations.

. . . If a political generation is not the same as a biological generation, it becomes all the more important to define the specific time span within which all who experience their formative years can be said to be molded into one distinct political generation. Without such a definition, it is impossible to classify individuals as members of one or another political generation with any precision, especially since few significant historic events "begin" and "end" with as much definiteness as World War I. Such classification cannot be done on an ad hoc basis. If the ad hoc method is attempted, it may properly be suspected that generational differences are being used as a deus ex machina in much the same way that differences in national character are sometimes invoked when there seems to be no other explanation of some political phenomenon. On the other hand, since the concept of political generation is closely related to the process of social change, any arbitrary choice of time span is likely to violate the complexity of reality. The actual time span involved in a generation will differ substantially in periods in which the process of social change is more rapid or less rapid. Karl Mannheim (1928) suggested that whether a new generation appears every year, every thirty years, or every hundred years, or whether it emerges rhythmically at all, depends entirely on the specific social context. This variability, of course, is merely one aspect of the general problem of applying ideal types to concrete situations. All concepts of comparative analysis must be defined in time and space if they are to be of any use in clarifying reality. This is especially true of the concept of political generation, since membership in the same generation involves common location in time and space. In twentieth-century Western society, in which social change is not only rapid but cataclysmic, the time span of a political generation is considerably shorter than in more stable societies. The most reasonable estimate for the time span of a political generation in twentieth-century Western society is probably ten to fifteen years. In twentieth-century non-Western societies experiencing revolutionary social, economic, and political changes, this time span may be even shorter.

... Although the spatial span of a political generation is difficult to define with precision, it is clear that many coevals in the human race are not members of the same generation. Those whose formative experiences are fundamentally different cannot be members of the same generation, even though they may coexist in time. There was, for instance, as Mannheim pointed out, no community of experience between youths in China and Germany about 1800. It could be argued that there is considerable community of experience between youths in East Germany and Communist China today, since their formative years are spent in similar totalitarian political environments. Indeed, such phenomena as the spread of nationalism and of industrialization indicate that the spatial barriers between generations may be breaking down, at the same time that more rapid social change is increasing the importance of the temporal barriers between generations. The effect of the latter development is to make communication between different political generations more difficult, while the effect of the former development is to increase the world-wide significance of this decline in ability to communicate. The implications of these long-range developments for meaningful communication within and among political systems are not entirely encouraging. . . .

Political personages nevertheless write, as did one Canadian leader, autobiographies with such titles as *My Generation of Politics and Politicians* (Preston 1927). Indeed, perhaps the most impressive evidence for the existence of generational consciousness in politics is the frequency with which it is articulated in the autobiographical writings of political leaders. These writings often demonstrate that, as Léon Blum put it, "a man remains essentially what his youth has made him" and that there is a special kind of communication, in politics as in other aspects of life, between members of the same generation. . . .

II GENERATIONS IN CONFLICT: SOME CASE HISTORIES

Heinrich von Treitschke

FOCUS ON THE MOVEMENT: THE GERMAN STUDENT UNIONS

Heinrich von Treitschke (1834–1896), the nineteenth-century German historian, did more than any other man to transmit the heroic nationalist spirit of the Student Unions to later generations. As professor of history at Berlin, as a journalist and member of the Reichstag, he contributed massively to the indoctrination of the German Empire in the supreme importance of being German.

Treitschke's best-known works are his eloquently pro-German lectures on Politics *(first published, 1897–1898) and his multivolume* History of Germany in the Nineteenth Century *(1879–1894), portions of which are reprinted below. Like most of his work, Treitschke's* History of Germany *is weakened from the standpoint of objective scholarship by the author's flagrantly partisan stance. This militant nationalism, however, does seem to give Treitschke a special insight into the minds of the passionately patriotic Student Unions of 1815.*

The German Student Unions (Burschenschaften) *described in this article were organized in 1815, first at Jena and then at other universities in the divided German states, to advance the cause of German cultural and political unity. They were stimulated by the writings of men like Arndt, Fichte, "Father" Jahn, and other nationalists of the older generation. Most importantly, they were inspired by the common participation of young Germans from many different German states in the famous Wars of Liberation against Napoleon (1813–1815).*

The unions were officially abolished by the Karlsbad Decrees of 1819, following a political assassination committed by a psychologically disturbed young Burschenschafter. *The Student Unions survived underground, however, and played their part in the German revolutions of the early 1830s and of 1848. The colors of West Germany's flag today—black, red, and gold—were the colors of the banners and sashes sported by the young* Burschenschafter *of 1815.*

Under the aegis of the new freedom of the press [after 1815] there now suddenly sprang to life in Weimar a great number of political newspapers. Irresponsible journalism, of a kind that could arise only among this cultured people, yet a power, for with it began the momentous invasion of the professors into German politics. Luden had

From Heinrich von Treitschke, *History of Germany in the Nineteenth Century*, vol. 3, translated by Eden and Cedar Paul (London, 1915–1919), 32–34, 37–40, 43–44, 50–61. Reprinted by permission. Original footnotes and subheads omitted.

founded his *Nemesis* while the war was still in progress, in the first instance in order to fight against the foreign dominion, and he now added an *Allgemeines Staatsverfassungsarchiv;* next came Oken's *Isis* and the *Oppositionsblatt* of Weimar. . . .

For years past Luden had been the favorite teacher in Jena. His lectures on German history were, as had formerly been those of Fichte and Schelling, the meeting place for the mass of the students. The amiable idealism displayed by his whole nature, the patriotic warmth and the ease of his delivery, secured for him a prestige among the university youth which remained unchallenged for forty years. Those who judged the well-meaning man solely from his books found it difficult to understand his brilliant success as a lecturer. His historical writings were poor in new ideas and even more lacking in evidence of independent investigation; while of the arduous mental toil which political science demands of its disciples he had so little idea that when no more than thirty-one years of age (in 1811) he ventured with much self-satisfaction to publish a *Handbook of Politics* stuffed with harmless commonplaces.

How differently from the dull and decorous *Nemesis* did the *Isis* set to work, the *Isis,* unquestionably the most remarkable political journal of our history, an incomparable specimen of learned folly. Though responsible for numerous extravagances, Oken had acquired a well-deserved reputation as a natural philosopher, but he brought to the political arena no better equipment than a genuine patriotic enthusiasm, a few vague democratic ideas, indefatigable pugnacity, and the childlike illusion that a free press could heal all those wounds which it had itself caused. "History," he exclaimed in his preliminary announcement, "make its way like a terrible giant across streams and rocks, across *loco sigilli* and artificial barriers, laughing at all devices to capture spirit and sense and to overthrow them when captured. All things are good and everything is permissible." His readers were to learn the sense and the nonsense of the time, its dignity and its meanness. He did not disdain even roughness, mendacity, and calumny, commanding in advance those whom he attacked to confine themselves solely to literary weapons for their revenge. The unceremonious appeal readily found hearers. All the hotheads of the learned world made assignations upon the great arena of this "encyclopedic journal." Beside zoological pictures and discussions (the only valuable matter which the newspaper contained), were to be found all kinds of university scandal and literary polemic; even a rancorous article from the *Edinburgh Review* attacking Goethe's *Dichtung und Wahrheit* was reprinted with unconcealed pleasure; there were also political essays, and numerous statements of grievances and complaints of alleged arbitrary acts on the part of the authorities. All this was in the tone of the taproom, in "Oken's manner" as people soon began to phrase it—impudent, tasteless, and full of mockery, so that almost every fresh number of the *Isis* aroused new quarrels. Since the rich stock of German superlatives proved inadequate, Oken called in the art of the wood engraver to his aid, having pictures of men with asses' heads, of geese, of cannibals, of Hebraic and clerical visages, or it might be a knout, a cudgel, or a foot raised to stamp on something, printed beside the names of his opponents. . . .

How could the students remain quiet in this marvelously excited little world? The great days of the Jena university had come to a close in the year 1803, and for long it had been impossible for Jena to compare with the intellectual forces of Heidelberg or Berlin; but the glories of past days continued to cleave to the name, and the unrestrained liberty of Jena student life had always been renowned among the German youth. "And in Jenè live we benè" ran the old student's song. There was no other university town in which the dominance of the students was so complete; as late as the 1790s they had on one occasion trooped out to remove to Erfurt, and returned in triumph when the alarmed authorities had yielded to all their wishes. Contrasting strongly with courtly Leipzig, life in Jena continued to exhibit a rough, primitive, and youthful tone, in correspondence with the simple customs of the country. Just as the Ziegenhain cudgel, at that time the inseparable companion of the German student, was to be obtained in perfection only from the Saale valley, so also the pithy Jena regulations were highly esteemed in every students' club and dueling place throughout Germany; many extremely ancient customs of the *Burschen,* such as the drinking of blood brotherhood, were continued in Jena on into the new century. All roughness notwithstanding, an atmosphere of idealism pervaded these noisy activities, a romantic charm which was altogether lacking to the clumsy coarseness of the Berlin gymnastic ground. How many a youthful Low German, making his student's journey to the

Fuchsturm and to Leuchtenburg, had then first become conscious
of the poesy of the German highlands. With what gratitude and joy-
ful enthusiasm did the Jena students make first-hand acquaintance
with Schiller's dramas in the Weimar theater. Under the foreign
dominion, the university flaunted its German sentiments undismayed,
so that Napoleon was once on the point of burning "the odious nest
of ideologues and chatterers."

It was inevitable that this patriotic enthusiasm should flame up
more fiercely when the young warriors now returned to the lecture
theater, many of them decorated with the iron cross, almost all still
intoxicated with the heroic fury of the great struggle, filled with ardent hatred of "the external and internal oppressors of the fatherland." This was by far the best generation of students that had been
known for many years, but these young men were unfortunately too
serious for the harmless fantasies and the exaggerated friendships
which endow student life with its peculiar charm. The urgently necessary reform of disorderly student customs could be effected only
by a generation far more mature than had hitherto been the average
of students, but in two arduous campaigns these chivalrous young
men had had such profound experiences that they were unable to
settle down once more into the modest role of the pupil; the danger
of arrogance and conceit, which was in any case in the atmosphere
of the day, was for them almost impossible to escape. Similar tendencies to Christo-Germanic enthusiasm had once before showed
themselves at the universities, in the days of the literary *Sturm und
Drang,* when the young poets of the Hainbund were devoted ad-
mirers of Klopstock's *Messiah* and of the heroes of the Teutoburger-
wald, and when they burned an effigy of Wieland, the poet of seden-
tary life. What had then been the motive impulse of a narrow circle
was now common to thousands.

How contemptible must the corrupt club life of the students necessarily appear to the strict-living new generation, hardened by cam-
paigning. There still existed far too much of the barbarism of the
old bullying times, although the humanism of the new literary culture had extended its refining influence even over university customs. Intemperance and debauchery often displayed themselves
with a lack of restraint which to us of today seems incredible; gam-
bling was practiced everywhere, even in the open street; and the
ineradicable German love of brawling so far exceeded all reason-

able measure that in the summer of 1815 among the Jena students, 350 in number, there were 147 duels in a single week. The homely popular drinking songs and travellers' songs of the tuneful days of old had almost disappeared, and the students sang chiefly lewd ribaldry or the lachrymose effusions of a dull sentimentalism which belonged to a far earlier literary epoch. With the disappearance of the Rosicrucians and other secret societies of the old century, there disappeared also their spiritual kin, the students' orders. The associations of students from the same province (*Landsmannschaften*), which had since then been revived, jealously supervised their closed recruiting grounds, being characterized by a paltry particularist sentiment which arrogantly rejected everything that lacked the true parochial flavor, destroying all vigorous self-respect by the brutal fagging system (*Pennalismus*). The freshman must not complain if an impoverished senior student should offer him blood brotherhood and an exchange of goods; the freshman must then give all that he had upon his person, his clothes, watch, and money, in exchange for the beggarly effects of his patron. One who graduated in such a school acquired the art of servility towards those above and arrogance towards those below.

How often had Fichte, at first in Jena and subsequently in Berlin, uttered vigorous protests against these disorderly practices. Among his faithful followers there was conceived as early [as] the year 1811 the design of constituting a *Burschenschaft* or association of German students. The philosopher approved the undertaking; but, knowing his men, added the thoughtful warning that the *Burschen* must avoid confusing what was medieval with what was German, and must be careful not to value the means, namely the association, more highly than the end, namely the revival of German sentiment. The students of Jena now associated themselves with these proposals of Berlin. They knew the seriousness of the profession of arms, and desired to control the rude lust for quarrels by the institution of courts of honor. During the war they had fought shoulder to shoulder as the sons of a single nation, and they therefore demanded the complete equality of all students, with the abolition of *Pennalismus* and of all the privileges which at many universities were still allotted to the counts' bench. But their ultimate and highest idea remained the unity of Germany: the power and the glory of the fatherland were to be embodied in one vast league of youth, which was to put an end to the existence of all the particularist student societies. . . .

It is easy to understand that a childish belief in the infallible wisdom of "the people" and a sentimental preference for republican forms were far more prevalent among the students than among men of maturer years. Like the majority of older liberals, the students desired representative institutions chiefly because they considered that the mainsprings of particularism were to be found in the cabinets alone. It was Carl Sand's opinion that if only there existed a constitution in every German land, there would no longer exist Bavarians or Hanoverians, but only Germans!

Yet during these first years of the movement there was little trace of morbid over-excitement. Pretentious, indeed, was the aspect of the students in their extraordinary Christo-Germanic rig-out, biretta, somber coat, and feminine collar; nor was their appearance rendered more agreeable by the adoption of the new customs of the gymnasts which soon made their way to Jena. But beneath the rough husk was a sound kernel. Greatly astonished were the authorities when the continuous warfare against university discipline, a warfare which had ever been the pride of the *Landsmannschaften,* now ceased of a sudden; and how much more refined became the whole tone of academic life when the songs of Arndt and Schenkendorf were heard at the drinking parties, and when a number of youthful poets, and especially Binzer of Holstein, were continually writing new and vigorous students' songs. Almost all the serious songs which German students sing today date from this period; even the students' inaugural song, the *Landesvater,* now first acquired its fine patriotic sense through some happy modifications. Christian piety, though in many instances too ostentatiously displayed, was for the majority a matter of genuine internal conviction; many of the young dreamers seemed as it were transfigured by their pious delight in all the wonders which God had worked on behalf of this nation. . . .

As early as the summer of 1814 there was constituted in Jena a society of arms to prepare its members by means of knightly exercises for the military service of the fatherland. In the following spring, the members of two *Landsmannschafts,* weary of the fruitless old activities, joined certain students hitherto unattached to any organization, and on June 12, 1815, the new *Burschenschaft* was inaugurated, in accordance with the ancient custom of Jena, by a formal procession through the market place. It was led by two divinity students from Mecklenburg, Horn and Riemann, and by an enthusiastic pupil of Fries, Scheidler from Gotha; these were all fine young fellows who had fought valiantly during the war. The first speaker, Carl Horn, who at a later date became widely known as the teacher of Fritz Reuter, remained until advanced in age faithful to the enthusiasms of his youth, and died in the pious belief that in founding the *Burschenschaft* he had been engaged in "the Lord's work." The new association immediately broke with all the evil customs of *Pennalismus,* and it was governed in accordance with purely democratic principles by a committee and executive officers appointed in open election; its court of honor reduced the practice of dueling within modest limits, and kept a strict watch upon the morals of its members.

A year after the foundation of the *Burschenschaft* all the other students' corps in Jena had been dissolved, and the *Burschenschaft* now seemed to have attained the goal of its desire, to have become a union of all the Christian German students. In these early days there still prevailed the good tone of a cordial patriotic enthusiasm. What an abyss separated existing custom from the roughness of earlier days now that the *Burschen* sang as their association song Arndt's vigorous verses:

> *To whom shall first our thanks resound?*
> *To God, Whose greatness wonderful*
> *From night of long disgrace is seen*
> *Forth-flaming in a glorious dawn,*
> *Who humbled hath our haughty foes,*
> *Who our strength for us renews,*
> *And ruling sits beyond the stars*
> *Till time becomes eternity.*

For the emblem of their league and of German unity, which this emblem was intended to symbolize, the *Burschen* adopted, in accordance with Jahn's proposal, a black-red-and-gold banner. Probably these were the colors of the uniform of Lützow's volunteers, and this force had also carried a black-and-red flag embroidered in gold. Some members of the *Burschenschaft* were indeed bold enough to maintain that in this banner were renewed the black-and-yellow colors of the old empire, embellished by the red of liberty, or perhaps of war (for red had once been the war color of the imperial armies). But the more zealous members would hear nothing of such historical memories, and interpreted their colors as meaning the passage from the black night of slavery, through bloody struggles, to the golden dawn of freedom. Thus it was that from out these students' dreams there came into existence that tricolor, which for half a century remained the banner of the national desire, which was to bring to Germany so many hopes and so many tears, so many noble thoughts and so many sins, until at length, like the black-blue-and-red banner of the Italian Carbonari, it became disgraced in the fury of party struggles, and, once more like the Carbonari banner, was replaced by the colors of the national state.

The intention of the *Burschenschaft* to unite all the students in a single association originated in an overstrained idealism, for the greatest charm of such societies of young men lies, in truth, in the intimacies of individual friendship. The invincible personal pride of the Germans would not so readily allow all to be treated on equal terms. To aristocratic natures, the general use of the familiar "thou," which the *Burschenschaft* enjoined, was uncongenial. Not alone the rude debauchees of the old school, but also many harmless pleasure-loving young men, were bored by the precociously wise and earnest tone of the *Burschen,* among whom prestige could be acquired solely by emotional eloquence, or perhaps, in addition, by good swordsmanship. Men of free and individual intelligence, such as young Carl Immermann of Halle, cared nothing for the opinion of the leaders of the *Burschenschaft,* holding that distinguished student chiefs are very rarely men of talent. The only resource against such opponents was dictatorial severity, and the narrowness characteristic of every new tendency (among young men at least) soon increased in the *Burschenschaft* to the pitch of terrorism. In Jena it proved possible for the time being to silence all differences of opinion, and the conceit of the *Burschen* now became intolerable. With important mien, the executive and the members of the committee strode every afternoon up and down the market place, deliberating in measured conversation the weal of the fatherland and of the universities; they regarded themselves as lords of this small academic realm, all the more because most of the professors exhibited for these youthful tyrants a quite immoderate veneration, compounded of fear and benevolence; even now, the leaders of the *Burschenschaft* looked forward to the time when their organization would rule all Germany.

Patriotic orations displaying passion and enthusiasm became more and more violent, already concluding at times with the triumphant assertion: "Our judgment has the weight of history itself; it annihilates." How many old members of the *Burschenschaft* went down to their graves inspired by the happy illusion that it was in truth their organization which had founded the new German empire. Half a century later, Arnold Ruge described the long struggle for unity and freedom characteristic of modern German history as a single great *pro patria* dispute between *Burschenschafts* and students' corps. Indisputably, many a young man of ability acquired his first understanding of the splendor of the fatherland at a students' drinking party, but the political idealism of those days was too formless to arouse a definitely directed sentiment. To the first generation of the *Burschenschaft* there belonged, in addition to isolated liberal party leaders like H. von Gagern, a great many men who subsequently displayed ultra-conservative tendencies, as for instance Leo, Stahl, W. Menzel, Jarke, and Hengstenberg. Voluble enthusiasm, hazy egoism, and the persistent confusion of appearance and reality, were unfavorable to the development of political talent. On the whole it may be said that from the *Burschenschaft* there proceeded more professors and authors, while from the ranks of the corps, the subsequent opponents of the *Burschenschaft,* were derived more statesmen.

For the present, however, the *Burschenschaft* was supreme in Jena. Its fame was disseminated through all the universities, where it attracted new students, and at Jena the number of students speedily became doubled. At other universities, too, *Burschenschafts* were established; in Giessen, for instance, and in Tübingen, where as long before as 1813 a Tugendbund had been founded to counteract academic brutality. Quite spontaneously there now awakened the desire to celebrate the new community at a formal meeting of all German *Burschen.* In dispersed peoples, the impulse to unity finds natural expression in such free social relationships, extending beyond the bounds of the individual state; in Germany, as in Italy, congresses of men of science, artists, and industrials were, like stormy petrels, the forerunners of the bloody struggles for unity. Among the

Germans it was the students who took the first step, and nothing can show more plainly the inertia of political life in those days. Long before grown men had conceived the idea of coming to an understanding about their serious common interests, among our youth the impulse became active to interchange their common dreams and hopes, and through the play of the imaginative life to rejoice in the ideal unity of the fatherland.

The centenary festival of the Reformation awakened everywhere among Protestants a happy sentiment of grateful pride. In these days even Goethe sang: "Ever in art and science shall my voice of protest rise." The students, in especial, were affected by this mood of the time, because their minds were still influenced by the Christian Protestant enthusiasm of the War of Liberation. When the idea of a great fraternal festival of the German *Burschen* was first mooted in Jahn's circle, the Jena *Burschenschaft* resolved to postpone the day of assembly to the eighteenth day of "the moon of victory" in the year 1817, in order to combine the centenary festival of the Reformation with the customary annual commemoration of the battle of Leipzig. Arminius, Luther, Scharnhorst, all the great figures of those who led Germanism in the struggle against foreign encroachments, became fused into a single image in the conceptions of these young hotheads. To the more revolutionary spirits, Luther seemed a republican hero, a precursor of the free "conviction." In a commemorative pamphlet by Carl Sand, which was circulated among the students, the evangelical doctrine of Christian freedom was fantastically intertwined with modern democratic notions. "The leading idea of our festival," wrote Sand, "is that we are consecrated to priesthood through baptism, that we are all free and equal. From of old there have ever been three primal enemies of our German nationality: the Romans, monasticism, and militarism." By this attitude, the universally German character of the festival was from the first impaired. The Catholic universities of the highlands, which in any case had as yet no regular intercourse on the part of their students with those of North Germany, could not receive an invitation; the *Burschen* of Freiburg had to light their fires of victory on the eighteenth of October by themselves, on the Wartenberg near Donaueschingen. The Austrian universities did not come into the question at all, for they were quite aloof from the

German students' customs, and, with the exception of the Transylvanian Saxons and a few Hungarians, hardly any Austrians studied in Germany. Even in the Prussian universities, the *Burschenschaft* had as yet secured so few adherents that Berlin was the only one to accept the invitation. The consequence was that at the festival of the national battle the students of the two states which alone had fought at Leipzig in the cause of freedom were almost unrepresented, and all the extraordinary fables with which the liberals of the Rhenish Confederate lands were accustomed to adorn the history of the War of Liberation found free currency.

Long in advance, and with vigorous trumpeting, the press had heralded the great day. A free assembly of Germans from all parts, meeting solely on behalf of the fatherland, was to this generation a phenomenon so astounding as to seem almost more important than the world-shaking experiences of recent years. During October 17th fifteen hundred *Burschen* arrived at Eisenach, about half of this number being from Jena, thirty from Berlin, and the rest from Giessen, Marburg, Erlangen, Heidelberg, and the other universities of the minor states; following the custom of the gymnasts, the vigorous men of Kiel had come the whole distance on foot. Four of the Jena professors, Fries, Oken, Schweitzer, and Kieser, were also present. As the men of each new group entered, they were greeted at the gate with loud hurrahs, and were then conducted to the Rautenkranz, there before the severe members of the committee to swear to observe the peace strictly for three days. Early on the following morning, a fine autumn day, "the sacred train" made its way through the forest to the reformer's stronghold. The procession was led by Scheidler, carrying the sword of the *Burschen,* and followed by four vassals; next came Count Keller, surrounded by four standard guards, with the new colors of the *Burschen* which the girls of Jena had shortly before embroidered for their austere young friends; the *Burschen* followed two by two, among them a number of heroic German figures, many of them bearded (which to the timid already sufficed to arouse suspicion of treasonable designs). Delight shone from every eye, for all were inspired by the happy self-forgetfulness of youth which is still able to immerse itself in the pleasures of the moment. It seemed to them as if today for the first time they had been able truly to appreciate the glories of their fatherland.

In the banqueting hall of the Wartburg, which the grand duke had hospitably thrown open, *God is to us a tower of strength* was first of all sung amid the rolling of kettle drums and the blast of trumpets. Then Riemann, of Lützow's yagers, delivered an inaugural address describing in emotional and exaggerated phraseology the deeds of Luther and of Blucher, and going on to exhort the *Burschen* by the spirits of the mighty dead "to strive for the acquirement of every human and patriotic virtue." The speech was not free from the current catchwords about the frustrated hopes of the German nation and about the one prince who had kept his word. As a whole, it was a youthful and obscure but thoroughly harmless outpouring of senti-mentality, just as vague and unmeaning as the new password *Volunto!* of which the *Burschen* were so fond. Nor did the subse-quent speeches of the professors and of the other students exceed this measure, for even Oken spoke with unusual self-restraint, warn-ing the young people against premature political activities.

After the midday meal, the *Burschen* returned to the town and went to church, the service being also attended by the Eisenach Landsturm; and after church the champions of the Berlin and Jena gymnastic grounds displayed their arts to the astonished Land-sturmers. At nightfall there was a renewed procession to the War-tenberg, opposite the Warsburg, this time by torchlight, and here were lighted a number of bonfires of victory, greeted with patriotic speeches and songs. Hitherto the festival had been characterized by a pleasing harmony, but now it became manifest that there already existed within the *Burschenschaft* a small party of extremists, com-posed of those fanatical primitive Teutons of Jahn's school who passed by the name of "Old Germans." The Turnvater had felt that this valuable opportunity for a senseless demonstration must on no account be lost. He had suggested that the festival in com-memoration of Luther should be crowned by an imitation of the bold-est of the reformer's actions, and that just as Luther had once burned the papal bull of excommunication, so now the writings of the enemies of the good cause should be cast into the flames. Since the majority of the festival committee, wiser than Jahn, had rejected the proposal, Jahn had given his Berlin companions a list of the books to be burned, and his faithful followers, led by Massmann, now determined to carry out the master's plan on their own initia-tive, a proceeding which the committee, desiring to keep the peace, was unwilling positively to prohibit. On the Wartenberg, hardly had the last serious song been finished by the *Burschen* surrounding the fires, and the true festival been brought to a close, when Massmann suddenly came to the front, and in a bombastic speech exhorted the brethren to contemplate how, in accordance with Luther's example, sentence was to be executed in the fires of purgatory upon the evil writings of the fatherland. Now had arrived the sacred hour "in which all the world of Germany can see what we desire; can know what is to be expected from us in the future."

Thereupon his associates brought forward several parcels of old printed matter, each inscribed with the titles of the condemned books. Tossed in by a pitchfork, the works of the traitors to their fatherland then fell into the infernal flames amid loud hooting. The parcels contained a wonderfully mixed society of about two dozen books in all, some good and some bad, everything which had most recently aroused the anger of the *Isis* and similar journals. There were burned the works of Wadzeck and Scherer, and, to make a clean sweep, those "of all the other scribbling, screaming, and speechless foes of the praiseworthy gymnastic craft"; copies of the *Alemannia,* too, found their way to the flames, with issues "of all the other newspapers which disgrace and dishonor the fatherland"; then, of course, came three writings by the detested Schmalz (while the chorus intoned an opprobrious pun upon the author's name), and the *General Code of the Gendarmerie* by Schmalz's comrade, Kamptz. Beside the *code Napoléon,* Kotzebue's *German History,* and Ascher's *Germanomania* (followed by a shout of "Woe unto the Jews"), there was burned Haller's *Restoration,* the choice of this victim being explained on the ground "the fellow does not want the German fatherland to have a constitution"—although not one of the *Burschen* had ever read this ponderous book. But even Benzenberg and Wangenheim, liberals both, had to suffer at the hands of these angry young men because their works had proved incomprehensible to the Jena journalists. Finally, an Uhlan warrior's pair of stays, a pigtail, and a corporal's cane, were burned as "fuglemen of military pedantry, the scandal of the serious and sacred warrior caste"; and with three groans for "the rascally Schmalzian crew" the judges of this modern Fehmic court dispersed.

The farce was indescribably silly, but no worse than many similar expressions of academic coarseness, and it demanded serious consideration only on account of the measureless arrogance and Ja-

cobin intolerance shown in the young people's offensive orations.
Stein spoke in very strong terms about "the tomfoolery at the Wartburg"; while Niebuhr, ever inclined to the gloomiest view, wrote with
much anxiety, "Liberty is quite impossible if young people lack
veneration and modesty." He was disgusted by this "religious com-
edy," by the ludicrous contrast between the bold reformer who had
risen in revolt against the highest and most sacred authority of his
time, and on the other hand this safe passing of fiery judgment by a
group of boastful young *Burschen* upon a number of writings of
which they hardly knew a line! At the students' assembly, on the following day, the young men made use of calmer language, being
at least more reasonable than their teacher Fries, who had left them
a written discourse of an incredibly tasteless character, turgid with
mystical biblical wisdom and Saxe-Weimar arrogance of liberty.
"Return," admonished Fries, "to your own places saying that you
have visited the land where the German people is free, where German thought is free. . . . Here there is no standing army to burden
the nation! A little land shows you the goal! But all the German
princes made a similar promise" . . . , and so on. Certainly Stein had
good reason for censuring the Jena professors as "drivelling meta-
politicians," and Goethe reason just as good when he invoked a
curse upon all German political oratory, for what could be expected
from the young when their revered teacher held up the four-and-
twenty hussars of Weimar as a glorious example for the rest of Germany! The same repulsive intermingling of religion and politics
which was displayed in Fries's speech, came to light once more in the
afternoon, when some of the *Burschen* hit upon the idea of taking
Holy Communion. Superintendent Nebe actually conceded the point,
and administered the sacrament to a number of excited and more or
less intoxicated young men—a characteristic example of that deplorable laxity which in time of trouble has ever distinguished both
the temporal and the spiritual authorities of the petty states.

Notwithstanding the follies of individuals, the festival as a whole
was harmless, happy, and innocent. When in the evening the young
men had said their farewells with streaming eyes, for most of them
there remained a lifelong memory, scintillating like a May day in
youth, as Heinrich Leo assures us. They had had a brotherly meeting
with comrades from the south and from the north; they considered

that the unity of the disintegrated fatherland was already within their grasp; and if only public opinion had been sensible enough to leave these young hotheads to themselves and to their own dreams, the good resolutions which many an excellent youth formed in those hours of excitement might have borne valuable fruit.

But amid the profound stillness which brooded over the German north, the impudent speeches of the *Burschen* resounded far too loudly. It seemed as if friend and foe had entered into a conspiracy to increase to the pitch of mania the sentiment of morbid self-conceit, that deadly sin of youth which corrupts its honorable enthusiasms, as if everyone accepted the boastful assurance of Carové, one of the Wartburg orators, who had extolled the universities as the natural defenders of national honor. With ludicrous earnestness the liberal newspapers delightedly hailed this first awakening of the public life of the nation, "this silvery sheen in our history, this blossoming of our epoch"; while, on the other hand, the old terror of the domesticated townsman for the students who used to beat night watchmen clothed itself in a political dress. A whole library of writings and counterwritings illuminated the extraordinary drama from all sides, raising this outburst of students' revelry to the level of a European event. It was natural that the heroes of the occasion should participate with justified pride in this paper warfare. The most faithful picture of the young people's hazy enthusiasm was given by Massmann in a long report of the festival, in which the stilted oracular phraseology unquestionably served to show how much that was un-German was after all concealed in the Jahnese "strong-manhood." "Although the gloomy winter night of serfdom," he begins, "still lowers over the hills and the streams of the German land, nevertheless the peaks are aflame, and the blood-red gold of dawn gathers strength." . . .

Unfortunately several of the professors who had attended the festival proved far more foolish than their pupils. In a typically coarse newspaper report, Fries did not hesitate to express plain approval of the fire-assize which had dealt with the writings "of some of the Schmalzian crew." To "many who discuss Germany wisely and unwisely," Oken, in the *Isis,* held up the Wartburg gathering as a brilliant example, availing himself of all the pictorial wealth of his goose-heads, donkey-heads, priest-heads, and Jew-heads, in order to pour

out fresh scorn upon the authors of the burned writings, whereupon
the Jena students, in a masked procession through the market place,
gave a dramatic representation of the *Isis* caricatures. . . .

At the court of Vienna the only feeling was one of alarm and
anger. The news from Eisenach led Metternich for the first time to
devote serious attention to German affairs, which he had hitherto
treated with profound indifference, for he recognized with terror
that behind the fantastical activities of these young men there
lurked the deadly enemy of his system, the national idea. He immediately declared to the Prussian envoy that the time had arrived "to
take strong measures [*sévir*] against this spirit of Jacobinism," and
he requested the chancellor to join with Austria in common action
against the court of Weimar. In the first moment of panic he even
desired the immediate recall from Jena of all the Austrian students
at that university. In the *Oesterreichische Beobachter* Gentz published a number of savage articles upon the Wartburg festival, an
artful compost of perspicuity and folly. Only with trembling, he declared, could a father today see his son depart to the university. . . .

Bolton King

FOCUS ON THE YOUTH LEADER: YOUNG ITALY

*Bolton King (1860–1937), an active social reformer since his college days at
Oxford, was a lifelong admirer of the Italian revolutionary Giuseppe Mazzini,
founder of Young Italy and one of the great leaders of the* risorgimento.
King's masterpiece was his two-volume History of Italian Unity, 1814–1871
(1899). *His most popular work, however, was his* Life of Mazzini, *a chapter
from which is reprinted below.*

*Mazzini, a one-time recruiter for the Italian Carbonari, organized Young
Italy in 1831, in the wake of the failure of the Carbonari in the revolts of 1830.
The objectives of the new youthful underground movement paralleled those
of the older revolutionary group, and those of the* risorgimento *in general.*

From Bolton King, *The Life of Mazzini* (London: J. M. Dent and Sons Ltd., Every-
man's Library Series, 1912), pp. 22–29, 36–40. Reprinted by permission.

Freedom and union were their goals—freedom from petty despots and Aus-
trian hegemony, union for the divided states of Italy. Young Italy collapsed
in the later 1830s, but Mazzini gave the rest of his life to conspiratorial and
propaganda work for the cause of a free and unified Italy. He lived to see the
day, though he found Cavour's constitutional monarchy of 1860 considerably
less inspiring than his own youthful dream of 1831.

The Carbonari had voiced somewhat fitfully the national protest.
And just at this time they made their final attempt at revolution. Early
in February 1831—just before Mazzini was released from Savona—
the insurrection broke out in Modena, and spread at once to Parma
and the papal province of Romagna. In three weeks the greater part
of the pope's dominions were free, and the insurgent army was marching towards Rome. . . . But they made two irreparable mistakes. They
did not face the facts; they failed to win the people. They were for
the most part, like the rest of the Carbonaro leaders, middle-aged
professional men, out of touch with the masses, possessed by the
dread that popular imprudences might scare the diplomatists, on
whom they built their hopes. Under an inspiring chief, the people
would have fought perhaps, as they fought seventeen years later,
when they drove the Austrians in confusion from Bologna. But the
leaders were not the men to touch their enthusiasm. They had, in
fact, miscalculated what the movement meant. These comfortable
men of peace flinched from the fact that Austria must be fought and
beaten. They had no stuff for a desperate guerilla fight, that meant
the wasting of the country, privation and disease and death, for an
uncertain hope that France might come eventually to the rescue. Still
less were they prepared to launch on a forlorn enterprise, where
friends were none and immediate disaster certain, that they might be
precursors of their children's victories.

Their failure, so consonant with all the later Carbonaro policy,
confirmed Mazzini in his belief that a new organization was needed
and new men to lead it. As usual, he saw only one set of facts. He
exaggerated the mistakes of the revolutionary governments, and left
out of his reckoning the unreadiness of the people. The insurrections
had failed, he convinced himself, simply because they had been
badly led. In the main, indeed, he was right. The revolution had been
in the wrong hands. The Carbonaro chiefs kept at arm's length
younger men, whose energy might have made up for their own un-

FIGURE 1. A charismatic youth leader: Giuseppe Mazzini, Romantic revolutionary and organizer of the "Young Italy" underground. (*Foto Carmelo Catania*)

forwardness. If the next revolution was to fare better, it must have these younger men to captain it, men of confidence and enthusiasm and fresh ideas, men with a message that would nerve "those artisans of insurrection, the people and the young." Mazzini had at this time a supreme faith in his generation; he had already written in the *Antologia* of "this young Italy of ours," so vigorous and cultured and warmhearted, that no new movement, however bold and difficult, was beyond its powers.

> *Place [he said now] the young at the head of the insurgent masses; you do not know what strength is latent in those young bands, what magic influence the voice of the young has on the crowd; you will find in them a host of apostles for the new religion. But youth lives on movement, grows great in enthusiasm and faith. Consecrate them with a lofty mission; inflame them with emulation and praise; spread through their ranks the word of fire, the word of inspiration; speak to them of country, of glory, of power, of great memories.*

They had been muzzled in the past; they must not be again. So rigidly did he insist on this, that the rules of Young Italy excluded from membership, except in special cases, all who were over forty years. Mazzini had no diffidence to curb the magnificent egotism of a design, in which he consciously destined for himself the leading part. As one of his closest friends of those days said, "his confidence in men was great and in himself unlimited." "All great national movements," he wrote in later years, "begin with unknown men of the people, without influence except for the faith and will, that counts not time or difficulties." It is worth noting that Camillo Cavour, five years younger still, was at this same time writing to a friend that "he would one fine morning wake up prime minister of Italy."

When we disentangle Mazzini's ideas from superfluous verbiage that sometimes wraps them, two leading principles are found to differentiate them from those of earlier movements—the principles, that, with his trick of making watchwords, he summed up in the phrase, "God and the People." The new movement must have the inspiration and power of a religion. Italy needed something that would shake her from the hopelessness of disillusion and defeat, something that would prove she "had a strength within her, that was arbiter of facts, mightier than destiny itself." Action must be roused by action, energy by energy, faith by faith—the faith that made Rome great and inspired Christianity and sent forth the armies of the Convention, the faith that makes the weak strong in the knowledge they are carrying out God's will. Mazzini had two arguments to persuade his countrymen to this believing and conquering patriotism. He hoped to fire them with his own superb faith in Italy and her destinies. He called up "that old name of Italy, hung round with memories and glory and majestic griefs, that centuries of mute servitude could not destroy." Twice had she been queen of the world; many times had she, the land of Dante and Vico, of the papacy and the Renaissance, inspired European thought. "Italy," he said, "has been called a graveyard; but a graveyard peopled by our mighty dead is nearer life than a land that teems with living weaklings and braggarts." Her task was not yet done; she had still to speak to the nations "the gospel of the new age, the gospel of humanity." He pointed Italians to "the vision of their country, radiant, purified by suffering, moving as an angel of light among the nations that thought her dead." Rightly he judged that men, who shared his faith, would never despair of their country. But he had a more sounding note to strike. He had the genius to see that he who would have men rise to high endeavor, must appeal to their unselfish motives, that only when some great principle calls, will they lift themselves to heroism and sacrifice of all that makes life dear. The effort to make Italy meant the loss of thousands of lives, meant exile and imprisonment and poverty, the blighting of homes and the misery of dear ones; and men would only face it at the call of duty. The Carbonari had no call; they came of a school that appealed to interested motives, and the appeal inevitably broke down in the day of disappointment and defeat. Mazzini offered his countrymen "a national religion"; Young Italy was no mere political party, but "a creed and an apostolate"; it taught that victory came "by reverence for principles, reverence for the just and true, by sacrifice and constancy in sacrifice." As individuals and as a nation, they had a mission given them by God. God's law of duty bade them follow it; God's law of progress promised them accomplishment.

The other principle of Young Italy was social reform. Earlier liberal movements had thought or attempted little for the masses, though at all events the recent rising in Romagna aimed higher than Mazzini gave it credit for, and had more of a democratic tendency than contemporary movements in France and England. Mazzini exaggerated the revolutionary impatience of the masses in 1821 and 1831; but it was true that such enthusiasm as they had, had been cooled by the disappointment of their hopes. Revolutions, as he said, had been Dead Sea apples to them. They would be slow to stir again, till they saw that the liberation of their country had tangible social results in store. The gospel of duty would rouse the cultured middle classes, but at this time he seems to have thought that the uneducated, downtrodden, priest and official-ridden masses could not respond to the higher call, and must be won by some visible prospect of relief from present evils. Pope Julius' cry of "Out with the barbarian" would not touch men, who did not see how every social injustice leant in the last resort on Austria, how dear food, conscription, all the petty tyranny, were fruits of the foreign domination, that sheltered the princes who misgoverned them. Till the masses felt this, there was no hope of a successful war of liberation. "Revolutions," he said, "must be made for the people and by the people, and so long as revolutions are, as now, the inheritance and monopoly of a single class, and lead only to the substitution of one aristocracy for another, we shall never find salvation." The cry of the poor, unheard by most Italian statesmen from his time down to yesterday, was ever with him.

> *I see the people pass before my eyes in the livery of wretchedness and political subjection, ragged and hungry, painfully gathering the crumbs that wealth tosses insultingly to it, or lost and wandering in riot and the intoxication of a brutish, angry, savage joy; and I remember that those brutalized faces bear the finger print of God, the mark of the same mission as our own. I lift myself to the vision of the future and behold the people rising in its majesty, brothers in one faith, one bond of equality and love, one ideal of citizen virtue that ever grows in beauty and might; the people of the future, unspoilt by luxury, ungoaded by wretchedness, awed by the consciousness of its rights and duties. And in the presence of that vision my heart beats with anguish for the present and glorying for the future.*

That they would rise in insurrection, he had no doubt. Once make them see whence sprang their wretchedness, where stood its remedies, once make them feel that "God is on the side of the down-trodden," the people of Italy would be again what they had been in the days of the Lombard League and the Sicilian Vespers.

Out of these principles—social reform as the immediate end of revolution and duty as its inspiration—Mazzini built up an elaborate political program. He loved system making and hardly apologized for it. You cannot have unity or harmony without it, he urged, and to a certain extent he had practical justification. It were better, as he said and as subsequent events proved, that the nationalists should argue out their differences before the time for action came, and not paralyze themselves by quarrels in front of the enemy. It was this want of a positive program, that was, he thought, largely responsible for the failure of the Carbonari. Their policy had hardly gone beyond the overthrow of the existing governments; and they had mustered under their flag royalists and republicans, conservatives and liberals, with the inevitable result that after their first successes they split their ranks and fell an easy prey. It were wiser, so Mazzini pleaded, to be few but united. "The strength of an association depends not on its numbers but on its homogeneity." But the principle was necessarily an intolerant one. It barred many a true patriot, who could not swear to the whole Mazzinian doctrine. For such he had no pity. In his view it was only fear, "the Almighty God of most politicians," that prevented the Moderates from accepting his position. "There can be no moderation," he said at a later date, "betwen good and evil, truth and error, progress and reaction." Unluckily truth to him too often meant adhesion to his own theories; and he could never forgive men, who, starting from his premises, could not follow his logic to the end, though, like most men who pride themselves on being logical, he was often singularly incapable of accurate reasoning. It was this intolerance that wrecked so much of his after life, that made him waste his splendid powers in fighting men, by whose side he ought to have been working. . . .

Mazzini returned to Marseilles, and found himself among the refugees who had escaped from Central Italy. He recruited a few young patriots among them, and with their help he began to give body to his schemes. In a small room at Marseilles the young Titans started, with nothing but their own sincerity and daring, to revolutionize Italy. [He wrote:]

We had no office, no helpers. . . . All day, and a great part of the night, we were buried in our work, writing articles and letters, getting information from travellers, enlisting seamen, folding papers, fastening envelopes, dividing our time between literary and manual work. La Cecilia was compositor; Lamberti corrected the proofs; another of us made himself literally porter, to save the expense of distributing the papers. We lived as equals and brothers; we had but one thought, one hope, one ideal to

> *reverence. The foreign republicans loved and admired us for our tenacity and unflagging industry; we were often in real want, but we were light-hearted in a way, and smiling because we believed in the future.*

In later life Mazzini looked back longingly to the freshness and enthusiasm of those days, before failure had disillusioned him or misunderstanding estranged him from his friends. When he was well and happy, all the charm of his nature—his radiant idealism, his warmhearted friendship, his contagious unselfishness—made him the beloved inspirer of the little band that worked under his orders. "He was," said an Italian of him at this time,

> *about 5 feet 8 inches high and slightly made; he was dressed in black Genoa velvet, with a large "republican" hat; his long, curling black hair, which fell upon his shoulders, the extreme freshness of his clear olive complexion, the chiselled delicacy of his regular and beautiful features, aided by his very youthful look and sweetness and openness of expression, would have made his appearance almost too feminine, if it had not been for his noble forehead, the power of firmness and decision that was mingled with their gaiety and sweetness in the bright flashes of his dark eyes and in the varying expression of his mouth, together with his small and beautiful moustachios and beard. Altogether he was at that time the most beautiful being, male or female, that I had ever seen, and I have not since seen his equal.[1]*

But sometimes even now overwork and impatience told on him, and he felt ill and exhausted. In such moods he must have been a trying man to be much with—irritable, exacting, requiring absolute submission from his fellow workers, angry if they thought well of men whom he disliked.

For two years the little band worked on, sowing the seeds of revolution. It was a heroic enterprise. A few young men, without birth or wealth to help them, and, except for their leader, of no great ability, were planning to change the future of their country and preparing for war with a great military empire. To an outsider it must have seemed a madman's dream. But their masterful chief had taught them his own faith; and they, and thousands of their countrymen after them, found in it the power, to which few things are impossible.

---

[1] This description was given to, and published by Mr. W. Shaen. There is reason for thinking it was written by Enrico Mayer, the Tuscan educationalist.

They worked with remorseless energy, month after month, corresponding with sympathizers all over the peninsula, planting lodges of Young Italy wherever a chance opened, drawing together the threads of conspiracy. They found abundant backing in Italy. Mazzini appealed to his followers there to work among the people by every road that the despotism left open, to bring children to school and teach them, to hold classes for men in the country districts, to circulate pictures and pamphlets and almanacs, which would insinuate patriotic ideas without exciting the suspicions of the police, to carry the cross of fire from town to town and village to village. "Climb the hills," he asked of them, "sit at the farmer's table, visit the workshops and the artisans, whom you now neglect. Tell them of their rightful liberties, their ancient traditions and glories, the old commercial greatness which has gone; talk to them of the thousand forms of oppression, which they ignore, because no one points them out." His appeal found a ready response. Hundreds of young Italians, fired by his own passion, gave themselves to the dangers and toils and the thousand small annoyances of a conspirator's life. It was no light call. "I know of no existence," said one of them in later life, "which requires such continual self-abnegation and endurance. A conspirator has to listen to all sorts of gossip, to soothe every variety of vanity, discuss nonsense seriously, feel sick and stifling under the pressure of empty talk, idle boasting, and vulgarity, and yet maintain an unmoved and complacent countenance. A conspirator ceases to belong to himself, and becomes the toy of anyone he may meet; he must go out when he would rather stay at home, and stay at home when he would rather go out; he has to talk when he would be silent, and to hold vigils when he would rather be in bed." And behind these petty vexations, which meant more to the Italians of that day than to a generation trained in strenuousness, lay the knowledge that discovery meant prison or exile, perhaps death. But they faced it with the courage of men who believed that the "wear and tear was smoothing the way, inch by inch, towards a noble and holy end," who looked to the day when through their labors their country would be lifted from the slough of misgovernment and low ideals. Life and everything they were ready to give for that. "Here are we," said Jacopo Ruffini to his fellow conspirators at Genoa, "five young, very young men, with but limited means, and we are called on to do nothing less than overthrow an established government. I have a presentiment that few of us will live to see the final results of our labors, but the seed we have sown will shoot forth after us, and the bread we have cast upon the waters will be found again."

Mazzini might well be sanguine, with men like these behind him. He looked to his literature to do the rest. The journal of Young Italy was, as he described it, "a collection of political pamphlets," each of the infrequent and irregular numbers consisting of a hundred to two hundred pages, badly printed on bad paper. Later on, it was set up by French compositors, who knew no Italian, and whose misprints gave him infinite concern. He himself did most of the writing. It was terribly diffusive often and wanting in precision, but his articles re deem their literary defects by the glow of noble purpose, that made them thrill their readers, and gave them a potency, that perhaps no other political writings of the century attained to. . . . The journal had a small circulation, and only reached a limited number of young educated men; it was indeed too literary for popular consumption. There seems to have been a larger demand for rules and instructions and popular tracts written by Gustavo Modena, afterwards to become one of the most famous Italian tragedians of his day. At all events there was a considerable contraband of printed matter, smuggled to Genoa or Leghorn or across the passes into Piedmont, inside barrels of pitch and pumice stone or bales of drapery or packages of sausages. So great became the demand, that secret presses were set up in Italy and the Ticino to supplement the output from Marseilles.

The results surpassed even Mazzini's sanguine hopes. The first lodges of Young Italy were planted at Genoa and Leghorn, and they spread thence to a good many towns of North and Central Italy. The chief strength of the society lay at Genoa, where the nationalist and anti-Piedmontese parties made common cause, and men of every class came in—nobles and commoners, lawyers and civil servants and priests, seamen and artisans. Outside Genoa the working men seem to have kept aloof as a rule; years had yet to pass before Mazzini's social teaching reached them. The recruits came chiefly from the young men of the middle classes, sons of the men who had had their importance under the French rule and had been cribbed and kept under since the restoration. Here and there a young noble joined; in Piedmont and at Genoa at all events there was a sprinkling of older professional and business men; a few priests welcomed a movement, which bore so strong a religious imprint. Everywhere the

scattered remnants of the Carbonari enrolled themselves. Buonar-
rotti, *doyen* of the conspirators, descendant of Michelangelo, friend
of Robespierre and Babœuf and Napoleon, attached his society of
the *Veri Italiani.* Early in 1833 Mazzini, it is impossible to say with
what accuracy, put the number of affiliates at fifty or sixty thousand.
Many a man, who came to the front in the later nationalist movement or in the first Italian parliaments, began his political life as a
member of Young Italy. Garibaldi, a young sailor who wrote verses,
just promoted to be captain in the Genoese mercantile marine, whose
fearlessness and charm of manner made him the idol of the men
under him, and who had already learnt from Foscolo a belief in the
destinies of Italy as ardent as Mazzini's own, met the chief at Marseilles and joined the society. Gioberti, who was teaching a tran-
scendental and literary patriotism to the novices in the archbishop's
seminary at Vercelli, sent warm words of encouragement to the
cause of God and the people.

Rolland Ray Lutz

THE GENERATION AS A SOCIAL MYTH:
THE VIENNESE ACADEMIC LEGION

*Rolland Ray Lutz (b. 1921), professor of history at Kean College of New
Jersey, took his master's degree at the University of Chicago and his Ph.D.
at Cornell in 1956. He is the author of a number of articles on German and
Austrian youth in revolt. The pioneering essay reprinted below is one of the
first detailed examinations of a specific youth revolt in the light of formal
generational theory.*

*The Viennese Academic Legion analyzed here was an experiment in stu-
dent power—an experiment that failed. It was a student march on the Vienna
Landhaus in March of 1848 that overthrew Metternich and triggered the revolution in the Habsburg capital. Throughout the revolutionary year, the stu-
dent-worker alliance spearheaded by the students' Academic Legion was the
most radical—and often the most powerful—force in Vienna. When the reg-*

From Rolland Ray Lutz, "Fathers and Sons in the Vienna Revolution of 1848,"
Journal of Central European Affairs 22 (1962): 161–173. Footnotes omitted.

ular army recaptured the city in October, many legionaries were killed on the barricades, imprisoned, or driven into exile.

About a century ago, the writers Ivan Turgenev and Fyodor Dostoyevsky viewed the appearance of a youthful, radical intelligentsia on the Russian scene in terms of a conflict between gnerations. The liberal "fathers," as parents, writers, educators, and salon habitués, had begotten the radical "sons." Whereas the fathers were moderate, drawing-room reformers, the sons were "nihilists," as Turgenev expressed it in *Fathers and Sons* or, as Dostoyevsky put it in *The Possessed,* they were "possessed." We owe to Turgenev and Dostoyevski, more than to any one else, the concept of "fathers and sons." "Fathers and sons" has become the symbol of cultural polarization expressed in terms of a conflict between generations.

Following the tradition established by Turgenev and Dostoyevsky, we shall discuss the Vienna youth movement of 1848 in terms of a conflict between generations, between "fathers and sons." There were two groups of revolutionaries involved in the Vienna revolution, an older group consisting largely of persons in their middle and later years, and a younger group consisting, for the most part, of persons who were of college or near-college age. It was the younger of these groups which touched off the insurrection leading to the Vienna Revolution of 1848. Immediately after the outbreak of the revolution these two generation groups engaged in a struggle for control of the Austrian capital, a struggle which plunged the city into a continuous state of disorder. Ultimately, these contending "fathers and sons," together with their revolution, went down to defeat in the ruins of Vienna.

Before we discuss the historical role of the conflict between Vienna's "fathers and sons," however, let us examine its character as a phenomenon of generations. Like Turgenev and Dostoyevsky, we are really talking about factions, parts of generations, rather than entire generations. The most obvious distinction between the two groups is, of course, that relating to age. Let us, nevertheless, keep in mind the somewhat metaphorical character of the concept, "fathers and sons." By it, we refer to two factions who conceive of themselves as being distinct, from the standpoint of generations. This mental attitude not only embraces young men and persons one biological generation older. It also embraces persons in intermediate biological generations who are attracted either to the so-called "younger generation" or the so-called "older generation." Also, at the top of the age scale there are "fathers" who, from the biological standpoint, must indeed be grandfathers. Finally, there are the eccentrics, the older men who, for one reason or another, associate themselves with the "sons," and the younger men who identify themselves with the "fathers." We must, then, guard against literalism and remember that we are dealing with two groups, one of which is only generally younger than the other, but which think of themselves as being distinct generations. A "generation" in this sense is, after all, a social myth with only some basis in fact. Like other social myths, it plays its role in the area of social psychology. It helps to impart unity and character to a group of heterogeneous composition and gives the group a historical impact different from that which it might otherwise have.

Let us consider the extent to which Vienna's myth of distinct revolutionary generations is anchored in any real age differential. Unfortunately, the enrollment records of the Academic Legion, the youth faction's militia, have not survived; or, if they have survived, neither this writer nor any other scholar has yet discovered them in the archives of Vienna. A search of the standard works on the revolution has, however, yielded 142 names of legionnaires or of other persons known to belong to the youth faction. These names include those of the known leaders, as well as those of obscure persons who are mentioned incidentally. The present writer has established the ages of only forty such persons, as of 1848, but he has discovered the student identity of another forty-eight persons. Of the forty persons whose ages have been established, nine are thirty-five years of age or older; another six range from thirty to thirty-four, and the other twenty-five are under thirty. To the latter must be added most of the forty-eight students of unknown age, since few of them are likely to be over thirty years old. Of these eighty-eight persons whose age can be estimated, probably only nine, or about 10 percent, are thirty-five years of age or older. This still leaves fifty-four persons, out of the original list of 142, to be accounted for. Of these remaining persons, twenty-four bear either a teaching title or the designation "Dr.," which indicates that they have completed their studies and are, for the most part, over twenty-five years of age. How many of these are beyond thirty-five, there would be no way of knowing. We are assured, however, by Eduard Suess, one of the leaders of the "Aula," the youth faction, that its membership consisted largely of students and young *Doktoren*. The doctor's degree, in the Vienna of 1848, indicated that the holder had completed his formal education in one of the colleges (*Hochschulen*). Since the title *Doktor* afforded the holder considerable prestige in the community, it was rarely omitted when any reference was made to his name. Between the doctors and the students, the academic world is heavily represented in our total list of 142 persons. There are forty-three *Doktoren* and college teachers; three former students who had failed to complete their studies; and sixty-one students. The names of the remaining thirty-five persons are unaccompanied in the sources by any reference to a college background. Granting that some of these thirty-five persons may have had a college background, a conservative estimate of the proportion of academicians among our 142 persons would be about three-fourths. This certainly would indicate that the students and alumni of Vienna's *Hochschulen* were in a majority in the youth faction of 1848. It would also suggest, however, that the Aula's traditional reputation as a "student" affair may be somewhat misleading, since students may well have constituted less than half of the membership. Information relating to the age of members of the Aula does, nevertheless, indicate that there is some substance to its reputation as a youth faction. The present writer would judge the bulk of the "sons" to be in their twenties and early thirties, with the heavier representation in the twenties.

In contrast to the "sons," the "fathers" range generally from their thirties to their seventies, a much longer span of years. Again, we should recall that there is some overlap between the two groups and also that old men often pass for "fathers." At the lower end of the "fathers" age scale there are such men as Theodor Hornbostel (33) and Alexander Bach (35). In the middle range there are liberals like Anton von Doblhoff-Dier (48) and Rudolf von Arthaber (53). And at the upper end, there are the older liberals like Franz von Sommaruga Sr. (68) and Ferdinand Colloredo-Mannsfeld (71). The "fathers," then, embrace more biological generations than the "sons."

By pointing to such discrepancies between biological generation and social generation, we have suggested that the latter is something of a myth which influences the thought and behavior of people. The character of "generation" as a social myth, however, can neither be established nor dealt with on the level of such circumstantial evidence, for we touch here on an attitude of mind. In order to identify this attitude of mind and see it at work, we must start with the words and thoughts of people; in the present case, of the Viennese revolutionaries of 1848.

During the first week after the outbreak of the revolution, Baron Adolf von Pratobevera, a well-known liberal, addressed an open letter "to the students of Vienna," i.e., to the Aula. Pratobevera urged the "students" to quiet down and cooperate with the older citizens for the peaceful realization of the goals of the revolution. A few days later, on March 18, Count Albert Montecuccoli, an eminent liberal during the prerevolutionary era, addressed the "students" in the following manner:

> *To you, gentlemen, is due the fame of having served as a heroic vanguard in the opening battles. . . . Gentlemen! youth is the time for enthusiasm and quick action. Manhood, however, is the time for enduring construction and circumspect accomplishment.*

On March 30 Baron Franz von Sommaruga Sr., the new minister of education, likewise addressed an Aula assembly and urged the "students" to return to their studies and leave the burden of reconstruction to the older generation. Perhaps the most interesting testimony to the existence of a myth of social generations is the open letter, of May 25, from Count Ferdinand Colloredo-Mannsfeld, the nominal commander of the Aula militia, to his charges:

> *Students! Answer freely and openly for your commandant the question which he . . . directs to you: Do you trust in me? . . . If your answer is "yes," then take this advice. . . . Let the legion dissolve itself generously, nobly, and without hesitation. This step will bring honor to you and salvation to the city of Vienna and the whole fatherland. . . .*
>
> *Do not ignore the voice of your well-meaning father, for you have cause enough to give me recognition. Do not ignore me, as you have done when I have brought to the attention of many of you how unjust it is to disturb the night's rest of our fellow citizens. . . .*

The reply of the Aula was framed within the context of the myth:

> *Herr Kommandant! Your open question demands an open answer. Indeed, street corners are not a proper place for a father to discuss and arrange*

family matters with his sons. Nevertheless, since you have chosen the public way, we shall do likewise. Neither the father nor the sons have any reason to shun publicity. . . . The Academic Legion does not dissolve itself. It stands or falls with the achievements of March 15 and May 15.

In the above cases, the members of the younger group were identified as "students," "youths," or "sons." Of these, "students" was the term most commonly applied by contemporaries to the members of the Aula. It is a well-known fact that Vienna's youth faction called its governing executive committee the Student Committee. The identification, in the public mind, of the Aula as a "student" faction gives it the character of a group which belongs to the so-called "younger generation." Clearly, the Viennese "fathers and sons" of 1848 functioned within the context of the myth of social generations. They thought of themselves and of each other as distinct generations, and this mental factor is much more significant than the purely biological factor of age.

There were historical roots to this attitude of mind. The two groups were products of fairly distinct historical developments, and it is this which set them off from one another. A large number of persons in the older group experienced their formative years during the 1830s, the decade in which there was a marked transformation in Austria's cultural life. During the years following the defeat of Napoleon, Austria's literature had been characterized by a flight from political and social realities into nature's mountains and forests, into the historical past, into the spiritual and emotional recesses of the soul, or into a make-believe world of prosperous, good-natured, fun-loving burghers. In the 1830s, however, the whole tone of Austria's cultural life changed:

The public spirit demanded a more substantial fare. Gone was the time when a naive audience devoted itself without much reflection to fairy dramas or to simple, lusty presentations of popular life. Alt-Wien sank with Schubert and Raimund into the grave, and then began the Vormärz *with its ominous sheet lightning.*

With the advent of the *Vormärz,* the pre-revolutionary period, Austrian literature assumed a political and social character. The herald of the new epoch was Anton von Auersperg ("Anastasius Grün"), whose *Spaziergänge eines Wiener Poeten* brought into public view in 1831 the myth of the sinister Metternich "system," with its spies, its police repression, its high tariff walls, its cultural "iron fences," and its snobbish officialdom. From this point on, Metternich and his "system" became the favorite enemy of the new Austrian liberalism, and as the 'thirties wore on the volume of literature critical of the regime mounted steadily. During this period, however, Austrian liberalism remained essentially a literary and drawing-room affair. It was the property of middle-class intellectuals and of certain aristocrats with commercial and industrial connections. There was nothing, of course, revolutionary about this movement. The substantial business and professional men of the Chamber of Commerce, the Reading Club, the so-called "Doblhoff circle," and other similar groups were not about to challenge the "system" in the streets of Vienna. It was in this atmosphere of middle-class, armchair liberalism that the liberals of 1848 received their political indoctrination. There was such a difference between the political attitude of Austria's first liberals and that of the student radicals of the 1840s that we must look beyond the influence of the adult liberals to discover the main source of student ferment.

That source may be found among the students of the German states outside of Austria. In the German universities, particularly in Protestant areas, the *Burschenschaft,* Metternich's famous *bête noire,* had flourished since the Napoleonic era. This confederation of student secret societies was the chief nesting place of German liberalism, democracy, and nationalism during the darkest years of reaction. Eventually, students from these German universities were attracted to the University of Vienna's medical school and also to the Vienna Polytechnic Institute.

During the decade of the 'forties nine secret *Burschenschaft* societies were organized in Vienna on the German model. Whereas the adult liberals were interested in mild reforms which would preserve the Austrian Empire and head it in the direction of a liberal, constitutional monarchy, these secret student groups desired fundamental changes. They wanted to democratize Austria's German provinces and incorporate them, in concert with the other German states, into a democratic Greater Germany. It is not surprising, then, that the two slogans which came to the fore in the Vienna radical movement of 1848 were "universal suffrage" and "intrinsic union with Germany."

When the revolution broke in March of 1848 Vienna's *Burschen-*

schaften were heavily involved. In fact, two of them, the Arminia and the Liberalia, presided over the birth of the youth faction in March 1848 by sponsoring the student petition movement which brought the Aula into being. Shortly thereafter the *Burschenschaft* societies merged with the Vienna youth faction of 1848. The Aula, in turn, assumed in modified form the nationalistic accoutrements of the *Burschenschaft:* uniforms with national implications; German tricolor insignia such as cockades, flags, and sashes; *Burschen* songs like the "Fuchslied"; national hymns like E. M. Arndt's "Was ist des deutschen Vaterland?" In sum, the radicalism of the "sons" bore the marks of the cult, complete with dogma, symbols, vestments, hymns, rituals, and mystical fervor. Like their Russian counterparts of a decade later, many of Vienna's sons were "possessed."

The Russian novelists Turgenev and Dostoyevsky have yielded a further insight into the phenomenon of generations. Namely, they have revealed that social antagonism was involved in the radicalism of the "sons." Some of them were of the settled, prosperous classes; but the integral radicals, like Basarov in *Fathers and Sons,* and Shatov, the Virginskys, the Shigalov in *The Possessed,* were really social misfits of lower-class origin. This impression is borne out by the philosopher and intellectual historian, Nicholas Berdayev. Berdayev notes that in the 'sixties an intellectual proletariat became an important addition to the Russian scene.

It is also likely that in the Vienna of 1848 an intellectual proletariat played a role in the conflict of generations. This conviction is based on an examination of the University of Vienna matriculation rolls for the years 1845/46–1847/48. Out of 1899 students who matriculated during those three academic years, 743, or about 39 percent, were classified as "poor" (*arm*) and were relieved of all tuition requirements. Obviously, many of the students who took part in the Viennese youth movement of 1848 must have come from backgrounds which involved economic hardship.

Since the matriculation rolls also give the profession of the parent, we have tried to ascertain the social origin of the students in the above sample. The two largest professional categories were: medium and small business, with 409 students, or about 22 percent; and handicrafts, with 399 students, or 21 percent. Thirty students, about $1^1/2$ percent, listed some form of unskilled labor. The combined figure of 838 students, approximately 44 percent, then, would represent the proportion which came largely from a shopkeeper, handicraft, or laboring background. There were also 55 peasants, representing about 3 percent of our sample. Even if these figures are not completely reliable, because of the obscurity of some of the terms used to designate the profession of the parent, they should convince us that many of Vienna's "sons" of 1848 were of lower-class origin.

This conviction is further strengthened by the knowledge that there grew up during the revolution a close alliance between the Aula and the "little burghers" and workers of the Vienna suburbs. What could be more natural than the assumption of leadership over the Vienna masses by the educated sons of provincial shopkeepers and artisans? In fact, large numbers of these students rented rooms in the homes of the poorer suburbanites. Many Aula members, therefore, not only shared a common social background with the lower classes of the suburbs, but they knew Vienna's *Kleinbürger* and workers personally as landlords and as daily associates. Also, the nationalistic and democratic ideology of the "sons," their demand for German unification and universal suffrage, appealed to the emotions of the suburban masses. The "fathers," on the other hand, spoke for the propertied classes of the walled, inner city on behalf of law, order, restricted suffrage, and the preservation of Greater Austria at all costs, conservative issues which failed to arouse the enthusiasm of the lower classes. Demagogy, then, was a characteristic which separated the "sons" from the "fathers" and at the same time was the real secret of the "sons' " power in the Vienna of 1848.

Let us turn, now, from the general features of our subject, as a phenomenon of generations, to its specific role in the Vienna Revolution. The struggle of generations figured in the immediate origins of the revolution in the form of a conflict between the students and alumni of the Vienna *Hochschulen* and the liberal members of the University of Vienna faculty. During the early days of March 1848 a number of *Burschenschaftler* decided to sponsor a petition demanding freedom of speech, press, and education, fair public trials, representative self-government, and popular representation of Austria in a Greater German government. The climax of the undertaking was to be a giant rally in the university assembly hall, the Aula, on Sunday, March 12. When word of this leaked out, the fathers decided to try to check the impetuosity of the sons. On the night of the eleventh

FIGURE 2. The youth revolution surfaces: an Austrian student agitator harangues a Viennese mob during the revolution of 1848. (*Historisches Museum der Stadt Wien*)

the rector of the university ordered the doors of the Aula locked, and on the morning of the twelfth he assembled his faculty in emergency session. Students and alumni soon gathered by the hundreds and demanded to be admitted to the Aula. At this point Professors Anton Hye, Stephan Endlicher, and other liberal favorites of Vienna's students left the faculty meeting and attempted to bring the mob of young people under control. These professors gave the signal for the opening of the Aula, and after much confusion gained the ear of the assembly. They were able to forestall a march on the palace only by promising that the rector and a faculty delegation would carry the "Student Petition" to the emperor that same day. The young men reluctantly consented to the proposal but insisted that the professors confront them the following morning with the results of their efforts. On the morning of the thirteenth the professors had to admit to the reassembled demonstrators that they had not been granted an audience with the emperor. Discipline now broke down altogether. The sons streamed into University Square and formed themselves into marching ranks. When the professors tried to impede the procession, they were thrust aside.

At this point, Vienna's youth movement of 1848 emerged full-blown with its own group spirit and its own sense of direction. Henceforth, it defied all attempts by adult liberals to bring it under their control. The subsequent events of the thirteenth are well known. Between two and three thousand students and alumni streamed into the government district and demonstrated in the streets and courtyards until they were attacked by imperial troops. This was a turning point in the affairs of 1848, for the outraged citizenry sided with the young men, and the revolution was underway.

The students and alumni of the Vienna colleges, then, launched the city on its revolutionary career in 1848. But having destroyed adult authority, they were in no mood to have it reconstructed in any form. Consequently, the fathers were in for a surprise. They cooperated with imperial officials to liberalize the central government, and they took over the city government. All this was in vain. Vienna's armed, organized youth resisted all efforts to restore order, and they soon discovered that they could rely on the suburban mobs to assist them in this undertaking.

In late March Alexander Bach, Professor Anton Hye, and a number of other liberal jurists were entrusted by the Pillersdorff ministry with the task of drawing up a press law. The idea was to impose some kind of check on Vienna's newly liberated press, which was virtually running wild. In the name of "freedom of the press," Vienna's sons gathered on April 1 at the Aula and heckled Professor Hye while he tried to explain and defend the newly published law. The upshot of the meeting was that the sons burned a copy of the press law in University Square and sent a delegation to Prime Minister Pillersdorff, who finally agreed to withdraw the law. Neither on April 1 nor at any other time throughout the revolution were the fathers able to impose an effective curb on the press. The sons stood guard over the uninhibited expression of the printed word.

A crucial point in the fathers and sons contest came in late May. On May 25 Professors Hye and Endlicher persuaded the Pillersdorff cabinet that the only way to establish the authority of the government was to dissolve the Aula militia, the Academic Legion. Early on the morning of May 26 Ferdinand Colloredo-Mannsfeld, the titular commander of the legion, placed himself at the head of a loyal National

Guard company and marched to the university, where he tried to persuade the legion watch to surrender the Aula. When this and other attempts failed, Pillersdorf, apparently without consulting liberal leaders, sent units of the imperial garrison into the university district. This outraged even the liberals themselves, and when the mob poured in from the suburbs and began erecting barricades, virtually the entire city sided with the Aula faction. As a result, Pillersdorff suffered a severe defeat and was forced to recognize the legality of a shadow government, the Committee of Safety.

At this point the sons tried their hands at the business of government. The Committee of Safety was a body which enabled the leaders of the Aula to join hands with the leaders of the suburban guard companies in the organized control of the Vienna radical movement of 1848. Officially, the committee represented the companies of the National Guard and the Academic Legion. The city council was also represented by a delegation. Actually, however, the Aula had usurped the loyalty of most suburban guard companies, and these outnumbered the liberal city companies. In practice, the Committee of Safety was the alter ego of the Aula. The original members of the Student Committee stepped bodily into it, and their place at the Aula was taken by their alternates.

We shall not discuss the efforts of the Aula leaders and their suburban guard allies to play the role of a committee of public safety. Their radical shadow government regulated and controlled the public works program, together with its huge labor force; served as a bureau of standards to supervise the weight and purity of food; regulated and supervised the rationing of foods; controlled the police and militia forces. In other sectors of government, it interfered spasmodically with the operations of the regular organs. Its activities came to an end in August, when it was outmaneuvered and outwitted by the new Doblhoff ministry and was finally, on August 24, forced to resign.

From August 24 till October 6 the fathers had things pretty much their way. The sons preserved their Aula faction, with its militia force, and they were still the leaders of the suburban masses. But the public works labor force, which had been controlled by the Committee of Safety and directed on the spot by the Academic Legion, had been drastically reduced from its peak strength of about fifty thousand, and its remnants had been dispersed throughout the empire.

The fathers, on the other hand, were partners in the central government, and they controlled the city government and the National Guard high command, together with the guard companies of the walled, inner city. Also, they had at their disposal the Vienna garrison, should they choose to use it against the sons and their allies. And, last but not least, the Doblhoff ministry, which represented the Vienna fathers, commanded a majority in the newly created Reichstag. They seemed, therefore, to have the mandate of all Cisleithanian Austria, in contrast to the sons, who could speak only for the Vienna suburbs.

By September the movement led by the fathers had virtually ceased to be a liberal phenomenon and had become an antiradical alliance which included some elements which could only be labelled counterrevolutionary. Alexander Bach, Theodor Hornbostel, Anton von Doblhoff, and Ernst von Schwarzer, the cabinet members who spoke for the fathers, could hardly at this stage be called liberals, for their principal concern seemed to be arresting the revolution by any means at their disposal.

The sons were only waiting for an opportunity to challenge the fathers once again. Their chance came in early October. On October 6 the ministry attempted to dispatch units of the Vienna garrison to the Hungarian front to assist the imperial armies in crushing the Hungarian Revolution. When the troops attempted to depart from Vienna, they found their way blocked by the old combination of radical elements: the Academic Legion, suburban guard companies, and the suburban mob. For the first time since the March days, imperial soldiers fired on Viennese revolutionaries. The legion, the suburban guard, and the mob countercharged and defeated the regulars. These events launched Vienna on the October Revolution, a radical revolution within a revolution.

Following their victory over the imperial troops, the sons organized their guard allies and the suburban mob into a giant victory parade. Legionnaires, suburban guardsmen, artisans, and workers paraded captured soldiers and artillery pieces triumphantly about the streets of the inner city and then headed for the university with their booty. As they drew abreast of St. Stephen's cathedral, guard units from the inner city opened fire on them, and fighting ensued in and around the cathedral. The armed citizens of the inner city were soon defeated, and it was the city guard which took the initiative in apologizing and in suing for peace. The Student Committee coolly accepted the olive branch, but that did not end the friction between the Aula and the older nonradicals of the inner city.

On October 12 the contest between the fathers and sons was renewed when the commander of the National Guard resigned. The city guard companies proceeded unilaterally to elect Simon Spitz-hütl, a nonradical, as the new commander. When the Student Committee got word of this it countered with its own candidate, Wenzel Messenhauer. Ultimately, the Reichstag's Permanent Committee resolved the matter by making the Aula candidate provisional commander.

Though the non-radicals in the city Guard and in the city council once again bowed to the Aula faction, the underlying antagonism between the fathers and sons persisted. On the twenty-ninth Messenhauer sided with the nonradicals, after the Vienna suburbs had been attacked and largely occupied by the imperial regulars. He and a number of wavering elements voted with the majority of militia officers in favor of capitulation. The city council undertook negotiations with the besieging imperial generals, and Vienna appeared to be on the verge of surrender. On the thirtieth, however, the lookout in St. Stephen's tower reported that the Hungarian revolutionary army had attacked the imperial armies from the rear and was attempting to raise the siege of Vienna. When this was verified, the Student Committee demanded the immediate resumption of hostilities. Messenhauer refused and was promptly ordered to resign by the Student Committee. The latter had found a candidate in the arch radical, Fenner von Fenneberg, who was willing to resume the fighting. A compromise was reached, again through the offices of the Reichstag Permanent Committee, and Messenhauer was retained, with Fenneberg serving as second in command. The question of resuming hostilities, however, was not answered. When, on the thirtieth, the imperial armies advanced to accept the surrender of Vienna, they were fired on by certain radical militia units. The regulars promptly retired and bombed the city well into the night. On the morning of the thirty-first the bombardment was resumed and was followed by a full-scale assault on the city's walls. This time the imperial armies broke through the defenses, and within a matter of hours both the fathers-and-sons contest and the Vienna Revolution of 1848 came to an end.

Beneath the liberal-radical split of revolutionary Vienna was a
conflict of generations which played a dynamic role in the course
of events. This conflict was involved in the outbreak of the revolution. It played a part in the violence and excesses of the revolution
and in the failure of the liberals to capture control. Finally, it was involved in the destruction of the revolution itself. From beginning to
end, the phenomenon of generations was an integral and important
part of the Vienna Revolution of 1848. . . .

Daniel R. Brower

A SOCIOLOGICAL ANALYSIS: FATHERS AND SONS IN TSARIST RUSSIA

*Daniel Brower (b. 1936), who received his Ph.D. from Columbia in 1963, is
presently at the University of California at Davis. He has published books on
both French and Russian radicalism. Among his prime scholarly concerns,
he lists the cultural and social origins of radical intellectuals in both these
countries. The present essay, a clear outgrowth of this concern, is notable
for its solid grounding in the all-too-meager official records of the Russian
university revels of 1861 and their predecessors of the 1840s.*

*The "Petrashevtsy" of Brower's 1840s sampling were young Russians who
met in the shadow of tsarist autocracy to read and discuss such taboo subjects as western-style liberalism and socialism. Nicholas I's secret police
rounded them up in 1849 and dispatched most of them—including the young
Feodor Dostoevski—to Siberia.*

*The St. Petersburg student demonstrators of 1861 represented the crest
of a wave of youthful liberal idealism that flowered during the hopeful early
years of the reign of reforming Tsar Alexander II. Rigid university discipline
had been relaxed during those years, and young people had worked for such
larger social goals as worker education and peasant emancipation. In 1861,
however, while the serfs were being emancipated, reaction set in at the universities. In St. Petersburg in particular, student refusal to accept heavy-
handed new university regulations led to marches and demonstrations, to*

From Daniel R. Brower, "Fathers, Sons, and Grandfathers: Social Origins of Radical
Intellectuals in Nineteenth-Century Russia." © 1971 by Peter N. Stearns. Reprinted
from the *Journal of Social History* 2, no. 4 (1969): 333–355, by permission of the
editor and author. Original footnotes and tables omitted.

clashes with police and troops, and finally to mass arrests and the closing of the university.

By the middle of the nineteenth century, a major transformation of class structure in Russia was underway. Classes which had provided leadership for Russian society were declining, while new groups rose in their place. The reshuffling of classes produced considerable flux in the fortunes of individual Russians, some advancing rapidly, others slipping downward, still others obliged to enter new occupations in an effort to preserve their social and economic position.

These developments may have had an important influence on the origins of a movement of political and social protest which arose in Russia toward the mid-century. Sociologists have found that social mobility, both upward and downward, leads to extremism in political attitudes, either more conservative or more radical than the norm. Historians have even suggested that some radical and oppositional movements may have grown out of the feelings of insecurity and resentment of groups displaced from positions of power and prestige by new groups. The American historian David Donald has used this argument to interpret the origins of the New England Abolitionists of the 1830s. A similar line of investigation can be applied to Russia in the first half of the nineteenth century. In the period between 1830 and 1860, a sizeable group of radical intellectuals appeared, critical of traditional institutions and committed to a profoundly different social and political ordering of human life. Their beliefs and activities have been the subject of extensive study, but their background in Russian society remains unexplored. They have even been split internally into two generational groups, the moderate "fathers" of the early years and the revolutionary "sons" of the post-1850 generation. The former group was supposedly of predominantly noble background, the latter non-noble. But no historian has yet attempted a detailed study of the precise origins of all or a part of this group in order to determine what influence social background might in reality have had on their intellectual revolt from Russian society.

During the first half of the nineteenth century, the groups which had previously exercised or been the agents of authority were either declining or altering their function. In proportion to the total population, growing at a rapid rate, the Russian nobility was holding its own. In 1857, the male nobles represented 1.5 percent of the total male population. But the economic foundation of the landowning nobility, traditional support of the autocracy, was weakening. More and more, these nobles had to depend on the financial aid of the state; in 1833, 43 percent of the landowners' serfs had been mortgaged to the state, and by 1859, the figure had reached 66 percent. The Orthodox Church, protector of religious conformity and moral leader of the masses, was falling behind the rising population. One historian estimated that priests represented 1 percent of the population at the end of the eighteenth century. But by the mid-nineteenth century, they totaled only 0.5 percent (36,000). Another indication of the church's decline was the decrease in the number of seminary students, totaling 24,000 in 1807 and 17,000 in 1850. Even the army and navy—and one may suppose the officer corps as a whole—were slightly smaller in proportion to the population by the mid-century, falling from 2.4 percent in 1795 to 2.15 percent in 1857. Together with the small aristocracy these groups of landowning nobility, priesthood and officers stand out most clearly as the old elite of the empire. Though the evidence is not clear, they do appear to have declined in terms of wealth and perhaps numbers as well in the first half of the nineteenth century.

In their place, other groups were becoming more significant. The Russian state was the most potent force behind the changes in upper-class structure. In the eighteenth century, it had relied mainly on the participation of the landed nobility for the implementation of its policies. But beginning late in that century, it turned more and more to its own paid personnel, the administrative bureaucracy. Power brought prestige as well, for the state provided its bureaucrats and officers in the army and navy a very precise system of ranking through the fourteen steps of the Table of Ranks. Each rank had its title, which many Russians came to regard as a measure of social status. To a certain extent, the upper bureaucracy (eighth rank and above) assimilated the outlook and behavior of landed nobility. They were granted membership in the hereditary nobility (a right restricted after 1845 to the first four ranks) and thus could purchase estates with serfs. Some made full use of these prerogatives. Yet their careers were taken up mainly with state service, while men from the landed nobility ordinarily spent only a few years in the bureaucracy or officer corps—most frequently the latter—before retiring to their estates. There was thus a fairly clear occupational distinction between the two groups. Evidence of this is contained in a recent study of the mid-nineteenth-century bureaucracy. Out of a group of 129 top officials (top five ranks), one-third possessed no serfs at all, and only 22 percent of that elite group had over 500 serfs, a level corresponding to real landed wealth. It is true nonetheless that the bureaucracy was internally divided, especially in terms of wealth. Even the upper bureaucracy can be referred to as a separate group only in the general sense of possessing great power and pursuing an occupation specially rewarded in Russian society.

I have been unable to find figures on the size of the bureaucracy in the first half of the nineteenth century. It is likely that the growth of the bureaucracy following Speransky's reforms was rapid. In St. Petersburg alone, the number of bureaucrats increased from 5,400 in 1804 to 13,500 in 1832. There is also evidence suggesting that the bureaucracy was receiving more advanced educational training in the later years of Nicholas I's reign. Out of a group of 486 men entering the bureaucracy (exclusive of secretarial positions) between 1840 and 1855, 41 percent had received an advanced education of some sort. An important factor in the rise of training of the bureaucracy was the possibility of beginning service at a middle rank thanks to educational experience. The system of higher education was expanding its enrollment until 1848. The exclusive Tsarskoe Selo *Lycée* doubled its number of students in 1832 from 50 to 100. The five Russian universities increased their enrollment from 1,450 in 1836 to 3,400 in 1848. It is thus probable that the bureaucracy was increasing both in size and competence during the period 1800–1850 and that the upper bureaucracy was more and more replacing the landowning nobility as the single most powerful group in Russian society.

By contrast, urban Russia was less dynamic. The urban population of Russia did rise from 6.6 percent of the total population in 1811 (2.8 million) to 10 percent in 1863 (6.1 million). But to a great extent, the inhabitants of the cities continued to live the narrow, stagnant life of the old petty bourgeoisie. The large urban centers of Moscow and St. Petersburg were growing at a rapid rate (respectively, 1.7 percent and 1.6 percent annually). Industry, however, was still not an important factor in city life; in the 1860s, there were about 750 factories in Moscow, mostly small enterprises with fifty to sixty workers. The cities, primarily St. Petersburg, were just beginning to make room for the literary professions, with a few critics, novelists, and poets struggling to make a living solely off their writing. They quickly acquired a voice in Russian life far out of proportion to their actual numbers. On balance, both the state and the cities were producing conditions for the reorganization of social leadership in Russia. In the eighteenth century, the nobility, as remade by Peter the Great, was the most modern element in Russian society. But a century later, this was no longer the case. Thus, the relative decline of the landowning nobility and the rise of the bureaucracy represented one part of the second stage in the social modernization of Russia.

The appearance of a group of radical intellectuals paralleled these social changes. Its uniqueness lay not, however, in specific occupational traits, but in its structure of attitudes. The assimilation of Western culture in the form of science, art, literature, philosophy (and theology), and social theories had encouraged the growth of modern intellectuals, men committed to comprehensive values regarding life, society, and human progress, which went beyond their occupational interests. Among these men, there were some whose contact with rational, critical thought, especially liberal and socialist theories, had led them to deny the rightfulness of fundamental Russian institutions in the name of higher values drawn from Western ideologies. As a whole, they differed widely among themselves in their program for change and in their attitude toward the institutions of Russian society (family, class, Church, state). But the rejection of prevailing values and the commitment to Western-inspired ideologies marked these intellectuals as a special group, sufficiently distinct to be described as a "subculture." Its rise was as much a part of the modernization of Russia as the restructuring of upper classes. Its roots in Russian society, however, are still poorly understood.

This article explores the problem of the social origins of the new radical intellectuals of Russia by examining the background of a small group from the mid-century. Specifically, it presents biographical information on a group of 90 radicals active in St. Petersburg in the 1840s and 1850s—52 from the first decade, 38 from the second. The number is small mainly because the problems of selection for that period were great. Documentary evidence from a variety of sources—archives, memoirs, literary biographies, etc.—is available for a fairly large group of intellectuals. But only a small number appear to have been radical in their convictions. Generally, I have concentrated on the participants in the circle of intellectuals known as the "Petrashevtsy," active in the late 1840s, and on the student activists in Petersburg University in the late 1850s. We possess biographical information on both groups thanks to the assiduousness of the Russian secret police, who arrested and collected vital statistics on the Petrashevtsy (1849), and the Petersburg University student demonstrators (1861). Because the availability of documentary sources was a major factor in the selection of individuals, men from the Petrashevtsy and the Petersburg student radicals make up the largest part of my group. In neither case did I include all the individuals named in the police archives, some of whom were involved in the affairs by accident, curiosity, or some other extraneous reason. I also included radical intellectuals from both decades who had no part in these activities. As a whole, my group does not represent a "random sample" of radical intellectuals in mid-century Russia. The group from the 1840s comes closest to being an unbiased selection, mainly because Petrashevtsy were a wide assortment of men drawn into weekly meetings by the reputation for radicalism of the host, Mikhail Petrashevsky. The group from the 1850s is quite biased toward Petersburg University students. One can argue that the university was in the 1850s a seedbed for radicalism, but such an observation should be a conclusion, not a criterion for selection. With these limitations in mind, the reader would be well advised to regard the statistics that follow as at best suggestive, at worst misleading. In spite of their deceptive appearance of finality they are included in this article mainly to suggest a new approach to the study of Russian radicalism.

These radical intellectuals were not men drawn from the lower depths of Russian society. . . .There were no representatives among them of the "unemployed intellectual" who is supposed to play such a crucial role in radical movements in developing countries today. The formative years in the development of their new outlook were most frequently the years of schooling, the crucial period for almost one-half of the total group. The question of what precisely took place in those educational institutions is a subject which I will not examine here. From the point of view of their position in society, the students had little reason for discontent. They were highly regarded by other Russians (at least until the disorders of 1861), and could look forward with confidence to a financially rewarding and respected occupation after graduation. Almost all of the students from the 1840s did in fact go on to government service. Mikhail Petrashevsky, for example, graduated from the Tsarskoe Selo *Lycée* in 1839, completed his studies in St. Petersburg University in 1841, and went to work in the Ministry of Foreign Affairs where within four years he held the rank of Titular Councilor (ninth rank). It is true that among these students there were some who suffered economic hardship. Information on this is inconclusive. It is likely that this factor would have been more important in the late 1850s, when university enrollment was greatly expanded and there were no longer sufficient state scholarships for all who required them. On balance, however, there appears no reason to stress deprivation in the lives of these students. They were among the favored in Russian society.

There were those who did not fare so well and whose years of intellectual revolt were also years of hardship and bitterness. Some willed it so. The writers and artists (10 percent of the total), particularly the former, had chosen a career which guaranteed few comforts. The profession had still to make a name for itself in Russian society, and the rewards for success were meager. When Nikolai Nekrasov, the future radical poet, decided at the age of seventeen to abandon training for the officer corps for the sake of studies in the university and a career of writing, his outraged father cut off all financial support. As a result, he lived for several years in utter poverty. Similarly, after having completed Engineering School and begun work in the Ministry of War as a sub-lieutenant (twelfth rank), Feodor Dostoevski at the age of twenty-three abandoned his position to devote himself exclusively to writing. If poverty were not enough to make these writers feel the precariousness of their occupation, the government censors had the power to make their lives miserable. In this struggle for a place in society, there was ample cause for protest against oppressive Russian institutions. In the case of both Nekrasov and Dostoevski, the company of the critic Belinsky encouraged them to reject the old order and to search for a new order in Russia.

Though the evidence is meager, it does suggest that a few of the radical intellectuals in the professions rebelled in large part against economic hardship. For those whose salary was not supplemented by income from estates or investments, life could be a struggle against poverty. There is insufficient information on income for the group of the 1850s. Of the thirty individuals (bureaucrats, officers, teachers) of the 1840s who were in government service, two-thirds lived solely on their salary. This is not a surprising finding, for Russian bureaucrats frequently had no outside source of income. For example, out of a group of over 1071 nobles serving at all levels in the bureaucracy, almost one-half (504) possessed no serfs, and hence did not possess an estate. By itself, the dependence on salary did not indicate hardship. As low as the tenth rank, the yearly income (about 600 silver rubles) appears to have been adequate. All of the men in my group serving in the bureaucracy (25 percent of the total) and had reached that rank or higher before becoming radicals. But there were others whose financial rewards were not as satisfying. The small group of teachers (9 percent) included at least one case of poverty. Felix Tol', son of a Lutheran petty bureaucrat in Narva, had been able to complete his education at the Petersburg Pedagogical Institute. But though trained teachers such as he were greatly needed, the Petersburg military schools, where he taught Russian grammar, apparently paid him a poor salary. Among the officers (6 percent), too, hardship existed. Nikolai Mombelli, son of a poor noble landowner who was a former army captain, lived in the 1840s off his income as a sub-lieutenant in the army. He testified during his interrogation in 1849 that he was so poor that at times he could not give his family enough to eat. His poverty, plus "pride, the desire to defend my dignity [and] not to lower myself in the eyes of others," and "unpleasant incidents" provoked by clashes with his superior officers, were the factors he blamed for a "moral crisis" resulting in liberal convictions. On the whole, these cases of personal hardship were a rarity among the radical intellectuals.

But dissatisfaction with the Russian social and economic order could arise from unsatisfied expectations as well as from individual hardship. One of the striking characteristics of the group as a whole is their propensity to try to explore new career possibilities. Statistics cannot reveal these aspirations to achieve. Higher education

is a crude indication of a desire to do well. Out of the ninety individuals, only six (all from the 1840s) had not received, either before
or during their radical years, some sort of higher education. Some
were unable to complete their training. Dimitry Akhsharumov, educated first to be a naval officer, tried to complete his education at
Petersburg University but failed for lack of adequate funds. He testified in 1849 that in those hard years "I re-examined the entire
social order; that was the beginning of my utopian principles and
aspirations." Others too found military service stultifying, and sought
new interests. Vladimir Obruchev, who completed the Petersburg
Military Academy in 1858, the next year retired from the guards regi-
ment to which he had been assigned in order to write for the radical
literary journal, *The Contemporary.*

The dissatisfaction with governmental service was particularly
great under Nicholas I. His enforcement of autocracy throughout
Russian life and of a new orthodoxy, Official Nationality, was for
some intolerable. Even men who were not committed to radical
ideologies felt the artificiality of Nicholas' policies. Dimitry Miliutin,
future minister of war under Alexander II, was in the 1840s a teacher
in the Petersburg Military Academy and an intellectual by the
breadth of his reading and his contact with Western culture. He
noted in his diary that everything about him in Russia was tainted
with "hypocrisy and falsehood." Part of the problem was the great
gap between the aspirations of such men and the very limited possibilities for satisfaction in Russian society. Even in the hopeful
early years of Alexander II's reign, this tension was felt. Nikolai
Serno-Solovevich, in 1859 twenty-five years old and serving as court
councilor (seventh rank) in the Ministry of the Interior, retired from
government service in protest over the autocratic methods of the
peasant reform. In his case, liberal convictions made it impossible
for him to continue serving the emperor, though his own career
could not have appeared more promising.

The occupations and aspirations of the greatest part of this group
of radical intellectuals place them squarely in the midst of the new
social groups appearing in Russian society. Some at least felt un-
happy with their social position, but their discontent was due mainly
to their own vision of what Russia should be and what they personally wished to accomplish, not to individual social and economic hardship in living conditions. Their ambition marked them as

part of the more modern Russians. In terms of the literary prototypes of the period, they were closer to the "sons" than to the "fathers" in Turgenev's *Fathers and Sons,* and did not resemble at all Goncharov's tragicomic hero Oblomov, the ineffectual noble unable to accomplish anything. Their dynamism could not help but be frustrated at least in part, and in that may lie one of the reasons for their rejection of traditional Russian society. Well-paid, highly regarded positions in society were open to them. If their convictions obliged them to turn down these favors, some of the responsibility must lie with their educational experience during which these convictions were elaborated. That problem will not be dealt with here. But it does not appear that an oppressive society "forced them," through economic hardship and social abasement, to revolt. In comparison with the Russian population as a whole, they could have belonged to the privileged few of their society.

Their families were mainly upper class as well. . . . The distinction between provincial and service nobility differentiates between nobles who devoted themselves primarily to full-time service (army or bureaucracy) and those who spent the greatest part of their lives on their estates, perhaps after a brief period of service. Taken altogether, these statistics indicate that the radical intellectuals in both the 1840s and 1850s were in large majority from the nobility, 85 percent in the former decade, 73 percent in the latter. The decline of 12 percent between the two groups is significant, for it indicates the growing diversification in the social background of the radicals. But in neither the earlier or later decade did the non-nobles (often referred to erroneously as "raznochintsy," i.e., "men of various ranks") make up the majority of the families. In the 1850s, the decade of the supposed rise of the commoners, they represented only 27 percent of the group. The priests' sons were quite insignificant; Dobroliubov is the only representative of this class in that decade; Chernyshevsky is one of the two from the 1840s. The prestige of these two men is such that they have been assumed to represent the "typical" radical from the mid-century. My statistics would indicate on the contrary that they were atypical, at least until the 1860s.

The importance of noble background in the origins of the radical intellectuals stands out even more prominently when compared with the social origins of students in higher education. The importance of higher education as a common factor in the background of the group has already been emphasized. The institutions of higher learning were probably the closest thing to a "seedbed" for intellectuals in mid-century Russia, for they prepared their students in rational, analytical thought and brought them in direct contact with Western secular learning. The profile of the social background of these students serves thus to pinpoint peculiarities and similarities between the radical intellectuals as compared with a larger group of intellectuals. I was able to locate statistics on St. Petersburg University and on the Petersburg Pedagogical Institute. The striking fact is that in both institutions, sons of the nobility were never in those years as numerous proportionately as the sons of nobles in the group of radical intellectuals. The Pedagogical Institute was composed mainly of students from non-noble families. In 1840 and similarly in 1850, only 12 percent of the students were from noble background (17 out of a total enrollment in 1840 of 167, and 12 out of 195 in 1850). In both those years, the single largest group was made up of non-noble bureaucrats' sons: 27 percent in 1840, 28 percent in 1850. The second largest group were priests' sons, representing 18 percent in 1840 and 24 percent in 1850. The predominance in the institute of the non-noble element is close to the current image of the generation of radical "sons," but has no parallel in my group of radical intellectuals, either for the total group or for the group from the 1850s.

On the other hand, the composition of St. Petersburg University was very similar to my group. In 1841, 52 percent of the student body were sons of nobles (185 out of 353), and in 1859, 58 percent (585 out of 1026). The second largest group were the sons of non-noble bureaucrats, with 16 percent in 1841 and 19 percent in 1859. As for the sons of priests, they represented only 4 percent in 1841 and 10 percent in 1859. It would be an error to argue from these statistics that the university "produced" radical intellectuals, for the problem is far more complex. My selection from the 1850s, largely made up of university "activists," could be expected to have an inherent bias toward the largest group in the university, the nobles' sons. With these qualifications, the striking fact remains that my group contained proportionately even more men of noble background than the most important large center of higher education in St. Petersburg. This suggests that the major problem in interpreting the social origins of the radical intellectuals concerns the nature and composition of the noble families from which four-fifths of these men came.

The designation "nobility" is far too imprecise to be of use in determining the social groups to which the families belonged. It is much more significant to point to the fact that, of the 68 noble families, more than one-half (39) were from the service nobility. The head of the family in these cases had devoted his life to serving either in the army, or, more frequently, in the upper bureaucracy. Such, for example, was the experience of Aleksandr Serno-Solovevich, born in a noble family in 1804. He began working at nineteen in the Senate at the lowly fourteenth rank. But within twenty years, he was a court councilor (seventh rank) in the Ministry of War, and was able to send both his sons in the early 1850s to the elitist Alexandrovsky (formerly Tsarskoe Selo) *Lycée*. For the most part, these bureaucrats had not received specialized professional training before or during their service. Their competence, like that of Serno-Solovevich, was as general administrators. Only four out of the thirty-nine fathers from the service nobility were professionals: one architect and three doctors. The sons of all four, though, became very well known: the architect's son was Petr Tkachev, and doctors' sons were Feodor Dostoevski, Vissarion Belinsky, and Mikhail Petrashevsky. Belinsky's father served first as a naval doctor, then as a district physician in the province of Penza; Dostoevski's father was a physician in a Moscow hospital; Petrashevsky's father became a leading Petersburg surgeon and hospital administrator, member of the Medical-Surgical Academy. Yet the professional occupations are numerically insignificant among the service nobility; most were bureaucrats of the early nineteenth century, without higher education and special technical competence. Most too were without land holdings; of the thirty-nine, nineteen held no estates and only eight held estates with over one hundred male serfs (information on property is lacking for another seven). In this respect, the group was typical of the nobility in government service.

It is difficult to obtain a satisfactory picture of the families from the provincial nobility. For this group, position in life was defined partly by property holdings, partly by participation in the administrative functions reserved for the nobles. Most seemed to do their share in performing some government service and managing their estates competently. Out of the twenty-four provincial noble families, I could find no information on the property holdings of nine; for the remaining fifteen, eight possessed estates with less than one hundred male serfs, and seven held more than one hundred. This means that for one-half of the known group, income from their estates was so low that they had either to live very poorly, or to supplement their income somehow. The father of Nikolai Mombelli, for example, had retired from the army in 1818, apparently to live on his sixty-eight-acre estate with its ten male serfs in the province of Smolensk. But he reappears on the state records in 1823 as chief of police in a town in the northern Ukraine. Even the more prosperous landed gentry found the time for occasional service. The father of another of the Petrashevtsy, Vladimir Khanykov, served in the navy for a brief time until retiring at the age of twenty and returning to his father's estates, and 313 male serfs, to the south of Moscow. According to his service record, written in 1824, he served as district (*uezd*) judge between 1812 and 1820. On the whole, thus, what information I possess on the provincial noble families indicates that their activities conformed to the usual pattern.

It would be interesting to know in greater detail what a normal life represented for the average provincial nobleman. The social history of the Russian nobility has yet to be written. Scattered impressions of rural noble behavior and attitudes can be found in memoirs from the period. The evidence is not at all clear. The picture drawn of the father of the populist Petr Lavrov shows him to be a respectable and honorable pillar of society. From an old noble family (back at least six generations) with property in the northern province of Pskov, he was educated in cadet school and served in the army to the rank of colonel before retiring. He was a stern disciplinarian at home and loyal subject of the emperor—Alexander I in fact visited him in 1824. His religious convictions were sincere but limited to the "observance of ritual," excluding all "excessive religiosity." He was well read and kept a good library, including many works of the Enlightenment. Mikhail Saltykov, on the other hand, painted a somewhat different picture of the Tver provincial nobility, among whom he passed his childhood. The nobles he remembered were quite backward. They believed themselves patriotic by "carrying out the orders of the government or simply of their superiors" and remained oblivious of some higher form of allegiance to their country. In religious affairs, they were "Godfearing" but observed church practices and customs like soldiers performing a "simple duty." They were scarcely touched by the organs of what passed at the time for mass communication; in Saltykov's neighborhood, one newspaper received several weeks late was the sum total of periodical literature until his mother began receiving in the mid-1830s the literary journal, *A Library for Reading.* The extent of their ambition for their sons was education in military school and service in the officer corps. If this picture is at all accurate, such a traditionalist upbringing could hardly have exerted any positive influence on the formation of radical intellectuals. On the contrary, one would expect such nobles to resist any deviation from the well-established pattern of "home, school, and service." There is evidence that some did. Nekrasov's break with his father has already been mentioned. Yet there were other provincial nobles, rich and poor, who favored their sons' efforts to obtain an advanced, secular education. There seems little reason at present to attribute any importance to the influence of social background from provincial nobility.

But perhaps the economic circumstances of these nobles played some role in the protest movement of their sons. The economic decline of the provincial nobility could have had a significant influence on the social and political attitudes of some of their sons. Unfortunately, my material on change in wealth is very meager. I was able to find information on eight out of the twenty-four provincial noble families; of these, three had maintained their economic position of the previous generation, one was growing wealthier, and four poorer. For example, the family of the radical critic Dimitry Pisarev was slowly selling the estates with their 330 serfs left by the grandfather, but was still able to preserve a landowner's way of life. In the case of the father of the populist Nikolai Mikhailovsky, the decline was catastrophic. He was forced in the 1840s, after having served in the army and then as police chief in a town in his province, to sell his family estate and serfs, and moved to a provincial town. He had become a *déclassé.* His son, a child at the time, was unable to finish the *gymnasium* (high school), but had to go to one of the Petersburg technical schools, the Mining Institute, where he could receive full scholarship for education and upkeep. Perhaps, thus, in a few cases impoverishment of the family contributed to the rebelliousness of the son. But the opposite example is just as revealing. Mikhail Saltykov's family had done very well for itself. His father was from an old but declining noble family. He married the daughter of a well-to-do Moscow merchant (ennobled in 1812 for his large financial contribution to the war cause). His new wife had far more business sense than he, and took the family affairs in hand. She soon earned the reputation of a ruthless and determined manager, a "kulak-baba!" Within thirty years, the family holdings had risen from 255 to over 3,000 male serfs. In addition, she sent her sons off to elite noble schools to prepare them for state service where they, as she told one of Mikhail's brothers, might "attain a rank worthy of your ancestors." Having attained status, as measured in wealth, worthy of the aristocracy, the family was apparently eager that their offspring receive a title from the state of equal importance. What impact this ambition might have had on the sons is a topic I shall pursue below. But the data I have found on economic background does not suggest that this factor was of any real importance in the revolt of the radical intellectuals. The evidence is meager, and contradictory.

The changes in Russian society during the nineteenth century were producing many instances of personal success as well as failure. Within the bureaucracy, both were occurring. At the bottom ranks (twelfth to fourteenth), there were men of noble birth with little hope of attaining a position of any importance. Out of a total sample of 235 nobles at this level in the 1840s, 27 percent were thirty years of age or over, and thus had little chance left of advancing to a high level. But toward the top of the bureaucracy were men who had risen far above their modest origins. Among 180 bureaucrats at the fifth to the first ranks, 18 percent were non-noble Russians (sons of lower bureaucrats, junior officers, priests, petty bourgeois, etc.), and among 470 bureaucrats at the eighth to the sixth ranks, 40 percent were non-noble Russians. These men could have reason to feel proud of their achievement, while the lowly noble bureaucrats could find little satisfaction in theirs. Social mobility among the upper classes in Russia has not been mentioned in connection with the radical intellectuals. Turgenev's classic account of the "new men" in *Fathers and Sons* suggested some connection, for the author portrayed his Nihilist hero, Bazarov, as a man whose fatner had risen from modest origins as son of a priest to become an army doctor. Perhaps Turgenev was in this respect gifted with an artist's insight.

The material which I was able to find on the change in social status among the families indicates a remarkable degree of advancement from paternal grandfather to father. . . . As usual, I was confronted with a sizeable number of families for which no information was available—almost a third of the total (27 out of 90). But of the remaining 63 cases, 46 percent had experienced upward social mobility. On the other hand, there were only three families which suffered decline in position, and one which shifted from one occupation to another within the upper classes. On balance, then, these statistics suggest that social advancement was an important factor in the background of these radical intellectuals.

As could be expected, the state was the single most influential agent in these success stories. Out of the twenty-nine cases of upward mobility, twenty-three were the result of advancement within the state apparatus (including two within the army). Economic forces were responsible for four other cases, and the church for two. For some of the bureaucrat fathers, their rise came with great speed. The history of the populist Mikhail Mikhailov's father is a good example. Son of a serf (owned by the Aksakov family), the elder Mikhailov entered the civil service at the age of sixteen as a lowly copyist. But thirty-five years later, he was an important provincial administrator with noble rank, had married the daughter of the lieutenant-governor of the province, and was a landowner with his own serfs. How he attained this success is not clear; his marriage into the lieutenant-governor's family was certainly a great help. A more ordinary story of advancement is that of the father of the Petrashevets Nikolai Serebriakov. The grandfather was a junior officer in the army, but the father entered the bureaucracy. He began working at the age of seventeen in the Senate, with apparently no advanced education, as provincial secretary (thirteenth rank), and at the age of fifty-one had risen to the seventh rank and had as well a small estate with 27 male serfs. In a society offering comparatively few opportunities for social advancement, these men could feel satisfied at their accomplishment.

The situation was more difficult for those who wished to receive an advanced training in some professional field. To become a doctor, for example, one had to go to the Medical Faculty of the universities of Moscow, Kazan, Kharkov, or Kiev, or to the Medical-Surgical Academy in Petersburg. The student years could be difficult for young men from poor families, but the opportunity for a successful career as military physician or public health doctor was great for those who completed their training. The medical profession was especially attractive to sons of priests, who had easy access to the necessary language skills (Greek and Latin) in the church schools and seminaries. Mikhail Dostoevski, father of the novelist, and Grigory Belinsky, father of the critic, both left families of village priests to go to Moscow University to study medicine. The former left behind him, in the western Russian town of Bratslav, a brother who was village priest, three sisters who married petty bourgeois, and three other sisters who married petty bureaucrats. With the esteemed career as a doctor before him, he could feel that he was making a new and a far better life for himself than that of his family. In the Medical Faculty at Moscow University, he was probably only one among many priests' sons. A few years later, in the early 1830s, the single largest group of medical students were from the ecclesiastical estate (94 out of 279). Their families represented an infinitesimal proportion of the priesthood in Russia, but they were on the way to becoming among the first "professionals" of Russian society.

Even within the ecclesiastical profession, there was some slight possibility for advancement. Both Chernyshevsky's and Dobroliubov's fathers, sons of village priests, became important church officials in provincial cities. Gavrila Chernyshevsky was brought up in poverty, for his father, a village priest in the Saratov province, had died when he was very young. But he was able to attend the district school, then the seminary, becoming in the eyes of his contemporaries a "learned priest." He was called in 1817 to the city of Saratov to serve as a teacher in the church school. He soon became one of the leaders in the church administration in Saratov, acquired an impressive theological library, and kept company with the local nobility. Surely the fact that Nikolai Chernyshevsky was from a socially mobile family in the Orthodox Church is as important, perhaps more so, than the simple observation that he was the son of a priest and thus a "commoner."

Still, the interpretation of the effect of this social mobility calls for great caution. The portraits given above of successful Russians should convey some idea of the complexity of the statistics on mobility. They should also make clear that these fathers of radical intellectuals were right thinking and loyal subjects of the emperor. The successful bureaucrats seemed to tend even toward excessive conservatism and imitation of upper-class manners. Vissarion Belinsky noted once that "the bureaucratic estate in Russia plays the role of a chemical tranformer, through which people from the lower middle class, merchant, priestly, and even noble estate lose their coarse appearance and enter the landowner's estate." Feodor Dostoevski's father was just such a man; having worked up to a rank giving hereditary nobility, he purchased a small estate and so mistreated his serfs that they ultimately assassinated him. Even merchants felt the attraction of noble status. Isaak Utin, who fathered a whole pleiad of young rebels, became successful through trading and banking, first in Archangel and then in Saint Petersburg. He was rich, lived in a comfortable house in the center of the capital, sent all his sons to the university, yet apparently wished for more. In 1862, he somehow acquired the title of personal noble. In the midst of these conservatives, there were a few "deviants," such as Belinsky's father, whose liberal outlook marked him an outcast in provincial society. But men such as he were the exception.

There seem to have existed nonetheless differences between these "self-made men" and their new peers from old, well-established families. The former had earned their new status on the basis of their own efforts and merit, and they appear to have been conscious that their sons had to make a special effort as well to maintain or improve their social rank. Where evidence is available, it points to fathers pushing their sons ahead, or accepting from their heirs suggestions for new careers which other parents would have resisted. Chernyshevsky's father owed his position largely to his learning and did everything to see that his son would enjoy the same advantages. His son's path to knowledge was originally to include the Petersburg Theological Academy. But when Nikolai decided he preferred the university, his father agreed. Whether one calls this sentiment ambition or achievement-orientation, it was a quality which broke with the traditional preoccupation of upper-class Russians with status. Some of the sons brought up in such a family atmosphere might have translated ambition into rebellion. Their place was not so secure as that of the sons of older, upper-class families, try though they might to make it so. The young Feodor Dostoevski, in some ways the caricature of the socially insecure individual, responded to his father's urging to become the "best sort of person" by developing an inflated sense of noble prestige. One of his acquaintances as a student, from an old noble family, remarked later that he seemed to possess a "diseased social consciousness." But hypersensitivity could lead to the rejection of the manners and outlook at first aped; by the age of twenty-five Dostoevski had written "Poor Folk" and was reading Fourier. Without venturing further on the uncertain ground of psychological interpretation, I would suggest that social insecurity might be a factor conducive to the sort of intellectual revolt apparent in the young radicals. But in the case of these young Russians, the alienating effect of social advancement was apparent on the second generation, not the first. These few families represent only a tiny part of the "nouveaux riches" of Russian society in the first half of the nineteenth century, and the fate of the sons was certainly an exceptional development within the larger group. Still, the "father-son" argument which Turgenev initiated in his novel may have more meaning for the origins of the radical intellectuals than realized until now.

The soundest conclusion to be drawn from the assorted and imperfect data presented here is that intellectual revolt came mainly from the "upper classes" of Russia. The attempt to locate the time and circumstances when the ninety young radicals came to deny the justness of basic institutions of their society and to put their faith in a new order revealed above all that their revolt was only infrequently associated with oppression and hardship. They were men whose training was very advanced for the time, who had before them the possibility of respected and often well-paid careers, and who were in fact very intent on finding a meaningful and useful life. Some experienced real hardship, others suffered the humiliations of the weak in a society which favored the strong, but they were the minority. If traditional Russian values and behavior no longer satisfied these men, the responsibility lay above all with their own aspirations and beliefs, not with conditions around them. For every Chernyshevsky, there were many more sons of priests who followed loyally in their fathers' footsteps; for every Serno-Solovevich, there were many more young bureaucrats who continued to serve the emperor faithfully. Somehow, somewhere in the upbringing of this small group of rebels, there occurred a fundamental rupture with the beliefs and outlook accepted by their family, their class, their society. This problem of socialization, i.e., family upbringing, formal and informal education, would seem to hold the real key to the formation of the radical intellectuals.

The question of social origins is still important. Only by studying the background of the radicals can one come to appreciate fully how isolated they were in Russian society. Their families were among the socially favored few of Russia, not among the masses. But this fact was the reason as well why most could have access to a modern education and to the new ideas from the West. Advanced education was the exception, not the rule, even within the upper classes of Russia. Entry into educational institutions was difficult and interest in new careers was still not great. The fact that so many of the young radicals came from families of serving nobles is important, for their fathers were the men most aware of the utility and interest in obtaining a good education, who also had the financial means to support their sons, and who had schools readily available to them. The situation of the families thus included both the means and the incentive to push their children on. The Russian bureaucracy was changing, as was at least a small part of the country's urban society. The social origins of the radical intellectuals put them close to the "modern" elements in nineteenth-century Russia. . . .

Peter Loewenberg

A PSYCHOHISTORICAL APPROACH:
THE NAZI GENERATION

*Peter Loewenberg (b. 1933) received his Ph.D. from the University of Cali-
fornia at Berkeley and currently teaches at the Los Angeles branch of that
vast state system. His published pieces include psychological profiles of Nazi
leaders, as well as the present paper on the psychological shaping of the
Nazi birth cohort as a whole. The article reprinted below is as notable for its
wide range of evidence—ranging from medical records to popular fiction—
as for its evident psychoanalytic slant.*

*The generations of Germans that swept Adolf Hitler into power in 1933
have, as Loewenberg points out, been the subject of a great deal of post-
mortem analysis. Were the German people driven into the arms of Nazism by
the oppressive terms of the Versailles Treaty? By the inflation of the 1920s or
the depression of the 1930s? Or perhaps by their own "totalitarian personality"
as a people? Loewenberg's intriguing essay suggests that the German generation that came of age around 1930 received a unique psychological conditioning in childhood, due largely to the traumatic experience of World War
I. This conditioning, he believes, psychologically predisposed a whole generation to accept the kind of rule that Adolf Hitler came to represent.*

The historical relationship between the events of World War I and its
catastrophic aftermath in Central Europe and the rise of National
Socialism has often been postulated. The causal relationship is
usually drawn from the savagery of trench warfare on the western
front, the bitterness of defeat and revolution, to the spectacular
series of National Socialist electoral victories beginning in 1930, as
if such a relationship were historically self-evident. It is the thesis of
this paper that the relationship between the period from 1914 to
1920 and the rise and triumph of National Socialism from 1929 to
1935 is specifically generational. The war and postwar experiences
of the small children and youth of World War I explicitly conditioned
the nature and success of National Socialism. The new adults who
became politically effective after 1929 and who filled the ranks of

From Peter Loewenberg, "The Psychohistorical Origins of the Nazi Youth Cohort,"
American Historical Review 75 (1971): 1457–1465, 1467–1477, 1479–1480, 1491–1498,
1499, 1501–1502. Copyright, Peter Loewenberg, 1971. Original footnotes and tables
omitted.

the SA and other paramilitary party organizations such as the Hitler-Jugend and the Bund-Deutscher-Madel were the children socialized in the First World War.

This essay examines what happened to the members of this generation in their decisive period of character development—particularly in early childhood—and studies their common experiences in childhood, in psychosexual development, and in political socialization that led to similar fixations and distortions of adult character. The specific factors that conditioned this generation include the prolonged absence of the parents, the return of the father in defeat, extreme hunger and privation, and a national defeat in war, which meant the loss of the prevailing political authority and left no viable replacement with which to identify.

Most explanations for the rise of National Socialism stress elements of continuity in German history. These explanations point to political, intellectual, social, diplomatic, military, and economic factors, all of which are important and none of which should be ignored. The historian and social scientist studying nazism should be conversant with and well versed in these categories of explanation. The study of political leadership is also of unquestioned importance for the understanding of the dynamics of totalitarianism, and it should be intensively developed by historians as an approach to that understanding.

This essay, however, will focus not on the leader but on the followers, not on the charismatic figure but rather on the masses who endow him with special superhuman qualities. It will apply psychoanalytic perceptions to the problem of National Socialism in German history in order to consider the issues of change rather than continuity in history, to deal with social groups rather than individual biography, and to focus on the ego-psychological processes of adaptation to the historical, political, and socioeconomic context rather than on the instinctual biological drives that all men share. . . .

This new kind of history requires an understanding of the dual and related concepts of fixation and regression. Sigmund Freud, in a demographic metaphor of migration, once compared human development to the progress of a people through new territory. At those points where resistance is greatest and conflict more intense the people will leave behind its strongest detachments and move on.

If the advanced parties, now reduced in strength, should suffer defeat or come up against a superior enemy, they will retreat to former stopping places where support stands ready. "But," says Freud, "they will also be in greater danger of being defeated the more of their number they have left behind on their migration." Thus, the greater the strength of early fixations, the greater will be the later need for regression: "The stronger the fixations on its path of development, the more readily will the function evade external difficulties by regressing to the fixations—the more incapable, therefore, does the developed function turn out to be of resisting external obstacles in its course." As in Freud's migration metaphor, when an individual who has passed through the maturational phases of development meets with persistent and intense frustration, one of the means of coping with the pain and lack of satisfaction is to revert from the more highly developed stages of mental organization to modes of functioning typical of an earlier period. The falling back, or regression, will be to phases of psychosexual development that have left areas of weakness, where the maturational step has been marked by unresolved conflicts and anxieties. Arrests of development or points of fixation occur in sexual-drive organization, ways of relating to people, fears of conscience, persistence of primitive kinds of gratification and of reacting defensively to old, no longer present, dangers. As Freud formulated it in 1913:

> We have become aware that the psychical functions concerned—above all, the sexual function, but various important ego functions too—have to undergo a long and complicated development before reaching the state characteristic of the normal adult. We can assume that these developments are not always so smoothly carried out that the total function passes through this regular progressive modification. Wherever a portion of it clings to a previous stage, what is known as a "point of fixation" results, to which the function may regress if the subject falls ill through some external disturbance.

The concepts of fixation and regression may be best illustrated by an operational example taken from a clinical case. A German lady comes into psychoanalytic treatment because of intense marital discord and an acute telephone phobia that interferes with her work. She cannot speak on the telephone, breaks out into a cold sweat, becomes intensely anxious, and loses her voice. In 1943, when she was three years old, she experienced the bombing of Hamburg. She remembers the air raids, the burning and explosions. She was not evacuated. Her family lived near the city center. Her father was a fireman who was called to duty by a bell that rang on the wall of the house because the family had no telephone. The patient can recall being strafed by an airplane. She has no recollection, however, of any panic, fear, or rage. Her memories are affectless. They are clear but disassociated from any of the powerful emotions that must have been present in the child. Now, in a current marital crisis, her feelings of explosive destructive anger and fears of abandonment by a man who is important to her cause a regression. The symptom of the telephone bell symbolizes an earlier point of fixation when she was traumatized by fears of external disaster and internal loss. She now, as an adult, re-experiences all of the emotions that were buried and repressed after the childhood trauma because the later, adult trauma has mobilized the earlier point of fixation and caused a regression to the feelings of the child.

Returning to the larger historical case of the German children of the First World War, it is Germany's Great Depression, with its unemployment, governmental chaos and impotence, and widespread anxiety about the future that constituted precisely such an "external disturbance" as Freud describes. The early point of fixation was the First World War, when the peoples of Central Europe experienced prolonged hunger, war propaganda, the absence of fathers and often both parents, and the bankruptcy of all political values and norms.

The psychological symptoms of regression to phases of ego functioning "fixed" by the traumata of a childhood in war included responding to internal personal stress with externalized violence, projecting all negative antinational or antisocial qualities onto foreign and ethnic individuals and groups, and meeting frustrations that would otherwise be tolerated with patience and rationally approached for solutions with a necessity for immediate gratification. The political expression of weakened egos and superegos that fostered regression was manifest not only in turning to violence but most especially in the longing for a glorified and idealized but distant father who is all-knowing and all-powerful, who preaches the military virtues and permits his sons and daughters to identify with him by wearing a uniform and joining combat in a national cause.

. . . The seminal conceptual formulation of the generation as a force acting in history was established by Karl Mannheim in 1927 in his essay, "The Sociological Problem of Generations." Here Mannheim speaks of the human mind as "stratified" or layered, with the earliest experiences being the basis, and all subsequent experience building on this primary foundation or reacting against it. . . . Mannheim then structures a further "concrete nexus" of the generation in history as *"participation in the common destiny of [the] historical and social unit."* And such groups he terms "generation units."

> Youth experiencing the same concrete historical problems may be said to be part of the same actual generation while those groups within the same actual generation which work up the material of their common experiences in different specific ways, constitute generation units. . . . *These are characterized by the fact that they do not merely involve a loose participation by a number of individuals in a pattern of events shared by all alike though interpreted by the different individuals differently, but an identity of responses, a certain affinity in the way in which all move with and are formed by their common experiences.*

This means that those of a generation who experienced the same event, such as a world war, may respond to it differently. They were all decisively influenced by it but not in the same way. Some became pacifists, others embraced international Leninism, some longed to return to the prewar, conservative, monarchist social order, and the ones we are concerned with sought personal and national solutions in a violence-oriented movement subservient to the will of a total leader. What was politically significant in the early 1930s was the facility with which individuals of this generation moved from one allegiance to the other. Mannheim's point is that although the units of a generation do not respond to a formative crisis in the same way due to a multiplicity of variables, the overriding fact is their response to that particular event. Because of this they are oriented toward each other for the rest of their lives and constitute a generation. . . .

The concept of the birth cohort—that is, those born at the same time—implies common characteristics because of common formative experiences that condition later life. Character formation, the direction of primary drives, and the internalization of family and social values are determined in the years of infancy and childhood. Each cohort carries the impress of its specific encounter with history, be it war or revolution, defeat or national disaster, inflation or depression, throughout its life. Any given political, social, or economic event affects people of different ages in different ways. The impact of war, hunger, defeat, and revolution on a child will be of an entirely different order of magnitude than the impact on an adult. This commonplace fact suggests that the event specificity of history must be fused with the generational-age specificity of the cohort of sociological demography and the developmental-phase specificity of psychoanalysis and childhood socialization to understand historical change. In this sense history may be the syncretic catalyst of qualitative longitudinal life history and the quantitative data of sociological analysis.

Rather than proceeding with the story of the Nazi youth cohort chronologically and beginning with its origins, this essay will use what Marc Bloch termed the "prudently retrogressive" method of looking at the outcome first, and then tracking down the beginnings or "causes" of the phenomenon. This, of course, corresponds to the clinical method of examining the "presenting complaints" first and then investigating etiology. The outcome of the story in this case is the related and concomitant economic depression, the influx of German youth to the ranks of National Socialism, the political decline of the Weimar Republic, and the Nazi seizure of power.

The Great Depression hit Germany harder than any other country, with the possible exception of the United States. Germany's gross national income, which rose by 25 percent between 1925 and 1928, sank 43 percent from 71 billion R[eich] M[arks] in 1929 to 41 billion R[eich] M[arks] in 1932. The production index for industry in 1927–28 was halved by 1932–33. In the critical area of capital goods, production in 1933 was one-third of what it had been five years earlier. The very aspect of Nazi success at the polls in the elections of 1930 accelerated the withdrawal of foreign capital from Germany, thus deepening the financial crisis.

The greatest social impact of the economic crisis was in creating unemployment. By 1932 one of every three Germans in the labor market was without a job. This meant that even those who held jobs were insecure, for there were numerous workers available to take the place of every employee. The young people were, of course, the most vulnerable sector of the labor market. New jobs were non-existent, and the young had the least seniority and experience with which to compete for employment. To this must be added that the number of apprenticeships was sharply diminishing for working-class youths. For example, apprenticeships in iron, steel, and metalworking declined from 132,000 in 1925 to 19,000 in 1932. University graduates had no better prospects for finding employment. They soon formed an underemployed intellectual proletariat that looked to National Socialism for relief and status.

The electoral ascendancy of the Nazi party in the four years between 1928 and 1932 constitutes one of the most dramatic increments of votes and political power in the history of electoral democracy. In the Reichstag elections of May 20, 1928, the National Socialists received 810,127 votes, constituting 2.6 percent of the total vote and 12 Reichstag seats. In the communal elections of 1929 the Nazis made decisive gains. With this election Germany had its first Nazi minister in Thuringia in the person of Wilhelm Frick, a putschist of 1923. In the next Reichstag elections of September 14, 1930, the National Socialists obtained 6,379,672 votes, for 18.3 percent of the total and 107 seats. At the election of July 31, 1932, the National Socialists became the largest party in the country and in the Reichstag with 13,765,871 votes, giving them 37.4 percent of the total vote and 230 parliamentary seats.

This extremely rapid growth of Nazi power can be attributed to the participation in politics of previously inactive people and of those who were newly enfranchised because they had reached voting eligibility at twenty years of age. There were 5.7 million new voters in 1930. The participation of eligible voters in elections increased from 74.6 percent in 1928 to 81.41 percent in 1930, and 83.9 percent in 1932. In the elections of March 5, 1933, there were 2.5 million new voters over the previous year and voting participation rose to 88.04 percent of the electorate.

The German political sociologist, Heinrich Streifler, makes the point that not only were new, youthful voters added at each election, but there were losses from the voting rolls due to deaths that must be calculated. He shows that 3 million voters died in the period between 1928 and 1933. The increment of first time, new voters in the same period was 6,500,000.

In the elections of 1928, 3.5 million young voters who were eligible did not participate in the voting. "This," says Streifler, "is a reserve that could be mobilized to a much greater extent than the older nonvoters." He goes on to suggest that these young nonvoters were more likely to be mobilized by a radical party that appealed to passions and emotions than to reason.

The Nazis made a spectacular and highly successful appeal to German youth. An official slogan of the party ran "National Socialism is the organized will of youth" (*Nationalsozialismus ist organisierter Jugendwille*). Nazi propagandists like Gregor Strasser skillfully utilized the theme of the battle of the generations. "Step down, you old ones!" (*Macht Platz, ihr Alten!*) he shouted as he invoked the names of the senior political leaders from left to right and associated them with the disappointments of the generation of the fathers and the deprivations of war, defeat, and revolution.

> *Whether they are named Scheidemann and Wels, whether Dernberg or Koch, whether Bell and Marx, Stresemann and Riesser, whether Hergt and Westarp—they are the same men we know from the time before the war, when they failed to recognize the essentials of life for the German people; we know them from the war years, when they failed in the will to leadership and victory; we know them from the years of revolution, when they failed in character as well as in ability, in the need of an heroic hour, which, if it had found great men, would have been a great hour for the German people—who, however, became small and mean because its leading men were small and mean.*

The Nazis developed a strong following among the students, making headway in the universities in advance of their general electoral successes. National Socialism made its first visible breakthrough into a mass sector of the German people with its conquest of academic youth. The student government (ASTA) elections of 1929 were called a "National Socialist storm of the universities" by the alarmed opposition press. The Nazi Student Organization (*Nationalsozialistische Deutsche Studentenbund*) received more than half the votes and dominated the student government in 1929 at the universities of Erlangen and Greifswald. In the 1930 student election it also captured absolute majorities in the universities of Breslau, Giessen, Rostock, Jena, Königsberg, and the Berlin Technische Hochschule. Both of these student elections preceded the Reichstag elections of 1930 in which the Nazis made their decisive breakthrough into the center of national political life. Developments toward National Socialism among the university students anticipated by four years the developments in German society at large.

The comparative age structure of the Nazi movement also tells a story of youthful preponderance on the extreme Right. According to the Reich's census of 1933, those eighteen to thirty constituted 31.1 percent of the German population. The proportion of National Socialist party members of this age group rose from 37.6 percent in 1931 to 42.2 percent a year later, on the eve of power. "The National Socialist party," says the sociologist Hans Gerth, "could truthfully boast of being a 'young party.' " By contrast, the Social Democratic party, second in size and the strongest democratic force in German politics, had only 19.3 percent of its members in the eighteen to thirty age group in 1931. In 1930 the Social Democrats reported that less than 8 percent of their membership was under twenty-five, and less than half was under forty.

"National Socialism," says Walter Laqueur, the historian of the German youth movement, "came to power as the party of youth." The Nazi party's ideology and organization coincided with those of the elitist and antidemocratic elements of the German youth movement. The Wandervogel, while essentially nonpolitical, retreated to a rustic life on the moors, heaths, and forests where they cultivated the bonds of group life. The Nazi emphasis on a mystical union of blood and soil, of *Volk,* nation, language, and culture, appealed to the romanticism of German youth *Bünde.*

The Hitler Youth adopted many of the symbols and much of the content of the German youth movement. The Nazis incorporated the uniform, the Führer principle and authoritarian organization (group, tribe, *gau*), the flags and banners, the songs, and the war games of the *Bünde.* The National Socialists were able to take over the youth movement with virtually no opposition. On April 15, 1933, the executive of the Grossdeutsche Jugendbund voted to integrate with the Nazi movement. On June 17, 1933, the Jugendbund was dissolved and Baldur von Schirach was appointed the supreme youth leader by Hitler.

A number of scholars have interpreted the radicalization of newly enfranchised German youth in the years of the rise of National Socialism. The Nazification of the youth has also been variously attributed to the spirit of adventure and idealism, a lust for violence and military discipline, the appeal of an attack on age and established power, and the quest for emotional and material security. . . .

The historical demographer Herbert Moller, on the other hand, stresses the factor of cohort size in creating the preconditions for political turbulence in Germany in the early 1930s. He points out that the proportion of young adults in Germany was very high at this time as a result of the high birth rates twenty to thirty years earlier. "The cohorts of 1900 to 1914," he writes, "more numerous than any earlier ones, had not been decimated by the war." Moller shows that precisely this cohort had its ranks swelled by immigrants from the territories ceded under the Treaty of Versailles and by German nationals from abroad, especially from Eastern and Southeastern Europe. Close to 1.5 million immigrants entered Germany from 1918 to 1925, just when emigration to America was being curtailed by immigration quota legislation in the United States. By 1930, because of the depression, a reverse movement of re-emigration from America back to Germany occurred. As a result of these developments, in 1933 the age group from twenty to forty-five was the largest in German history and constituted the highest relative percentage of the German population of any period before or since. In the year 1890 this age group constituted 34.4 percent of Germany's population. In 1933 it peaked to make up 41.5 percent of all Germans. By 1959 the twenty to forty-five age cohorts had dropped to only 33.7 percent of the German people. "From a demographic viewpoint," says Moller, "the economic depression hit Germany at the worst possible time: employment was shrinking precisely at a time when the employable population reached its postwar peak."

There is ample evidence that this generation of German youth was more inclined toward violent and aggressive, or what psychoanalysts call "acting-out," behavior than previous generations. At this point the explanations offered for this phenomenon are inadequate in their one-dimensionality. To say that the youth craved action or that they sought comfort in the immersion in a sheltering group is to beg the question of what made this generation of German youth different from all previous generations. What unique experiences did this group of people have in their developmental years that could induce regression to infantile attitudes in adulthood? One persuasive answer lies in fusing the knowledge we have of personality functioning from psychoanalysis—the most comprehensive and dynamic theory of personality available to the social and humanistic sciences today—with the cohort theory of generational change from historical demography and with the data on the leadership and structure of the Nazi party that we have from the researches of political scientists, historians, and sociologists.

In the half century prior to World War I Germany was transformed from an agricultural to an industrial economy, and her population grew from an agriculturally self-sufficient forty million to sixty-seven million by 1913. This mounting industrial population made her increasingly dependent on the importation of foreign foodstuffs. In the decade preceding World War I, five-sixths of Germany's vegetable fats, more than half of her dairy goods, and one-third of the eggs her people consumed were imported. This inability to be self-sufficient in foodstuffs made the German population particularly susceptible to the weapon of the blockade. The civilian population began to feel the pressure of severe shortages in 1916. The winter of 1916–17 is still known as the infamous "turnip winter," in which hunger and privation became widespread experiences in Germany. Getting something to eat was the foremost concern of most people. The official food rations for the summer of 1917 were 1,000 calories per day, whereas the health ministry estimated that 2,280 calories was a subsistence minimum. From 1914 to 1918 three-quarters of a million people died of starvation in Germany.

The armistice of November 11, 1918, did not bring the relief that the weary and hungry Germans anticipated. The ordeal of the previous three years was intensified into famine in the winter of 1918–19. The blockade was continued until the Germans turned over their merchant fleet to the Allies. The armistice blockade was extended by the victorious Allies to include the Baltic Sea, thus cutting off trade with Scandinavia and the Baltic states. Although the Allies undertook responsibility for the German food supply under Article 26 of the Armistice Agreement, the first food shipment was not unloaded in Hamburg until March 26, 1919. On July 11, 1919, the Allied

Supreme Economic Council decided to terminate the blockade of Germany as of the next day, July 12. Unrestricted trade between the United States and Germany was resumed three days later, on July 15. . . .

The demographic and statistical data constitute an overwhelming case that the German civil population, particularly infants and children, suffered widely and intensively during the war and blockade. Public health authorities and medical researchers have compiled population studies indicating damage to health, fertility, and emotions from 1914 to 1920. These are quantifiable indexes of physical deprivation from which the equally damaging but much more difficult-to-measure facts of emotional deprivation may be inferred.

On the grossest level the figures show a decline in the number of live births from 1,353,714 in 1915 to 926,813 in 1918. The birth rate per 1,000 population, including stillbirths, declined from 28.25 in 1913 to 14.73 in 1918. . . .

Upon looking at the comparative statistics for neonates and infants, we find a decline in weight and size at birth, a decline in the ability of mothers to nurse, a higher incidence of disease, particularly rickets and tuberculosis, as well as an increase in neurotic symptoms such as bed-wetting and an increment in the death rate. In the third year of the war the weight of neonates was fifty to one hundred grams less at birth than before the war. In one Munich clinic in the year 1918 the females averaged fifty grams and the males seventy grams less at birth than in peacetime. . . .

The pattern of increased illness and death among infants and small children in Germany carried through to children of school age. Deaths of children between five and fifteen years of age more than doubled between 1913 and 1918. Using figures for 1913 as a base of one hundred, the death figures for this age group in 1918 were 189.2 for boys aged five to ten, and 215 for boys aged ten to fifteen. Among the girls the death rates for these age groups were 207.3 and 239.9 respectively.

Among the leading causes of illness and death in this age group, as with the younger children, were rickets and tuberculosis. Corresponding losses in size and weight relative to age are also recorded. The medical statistics demonstrate an increased incidence among children of gastrointestinal disorders, worms, fleas, and lice. Psychological indications of stress among school children include an "enormous increase" in bed-wetting, "nervousness," and juvenile delinquency.

The evidence for deprivation is supported from Allied and neutral sources. The British war correspondent Henry W. Nevinson reported from Cologne in March 1919 that tuberculosis had more than doubled among women and children and that the death rate among girls between six and sixteen years had tripled. Because the children were so weak, school hours were reduced from seven to two hours daily. He wrote, "Although I have seen many horrible things in the world, I have seen nothing so pitiful as these rows of babies feverish from want of food, exhausted by privation to the point that their little limbs were like slender wands, their expression hopeless, and their faces full of pain."

The British medical journal *Lancet* reported comparative figures derived from official German sources showing that the effect of food scarcity on the health of the German population was felt after mid-1916 but was stilled by skillful press censorship in wartime Germany. Among children from one to five years old the mortality was 50 percent greater in 1917 than the norm of 1913. Among the children aged five to fifteen mortality had risen 75 percent. . . .

World War I was the first total war in history—it involved the labor and the commitment of full energies of its participant peoples as no previous war had. The men were in the armed services, but a modern war requires a major industrial plant and increased production of foodstuffs and supplies to support the armies. Yet the number of men working in industry in Germany dropped 24 percent between 1913 and 1917. In the state of Prussia in 1917 the number of men working in plants employing over ten workers was 2,558,000, including foreigners and prisoners of war, while in 1913 the total of men employed had been 3,387,000.

In Germany this meant a shift of major proportions of women from the home and domestic occupations to war work. In the state of Prussia alone the number of women engaged in industrial labor rose by 76 percent, from 788,100 in 1913 to 1,393,000 in 1917. For Germany as a whole 1.2 million women newly joined the labor force in medium- and large-sized plants during the war. The number of women workers in the armaments industry rose from 113,750 in 1913 to 702,100 in 1917, a gain of 500 percent. The number of women laborers who were covered under compulsory insurance laws on October 1, 1917, was 6,750,000. The increase of adult female workers in Prussia in 1917 was 80.4 percent over 1913. The number of women railroad workers in Prussia rose from 10,000 in 1914 to 100,000 in 1918, an increase of 1,000 percent.

Another new factor in the labor force was the youthful workers. The number of adolescents aged fourteen to sixteen employed in chemical manufacturing increased 225 percent between 1913 and 1917. For heavy industry the corresponding figure was 97 percent. Many of these were young girls aged sixteen to twenty-one. This age group constituted 29 percent of all working women.

That German women were massively engaged in war work was recognized as having resulted in the neglect of Germany's war children and damage to the health of the mothers. Reports came from government offices of increased injuries to children of ages one to five years due to lack of supervision. S. Rudolf Steinmetz evaluates the demoralization of youth between 1914 and 1918 as an indirect consequence of the war. He ascribes to "the absence of many fathers, the war work of many mothers" the damaged morals and morality of youth.

Many of the war-related phenomena under discussion were not unique to the Central European countries. The factor of a chauvinistic atmosphere of war propaganda was certainly present in all belligerent countries. The absence of the parents in wartime service was also not unique to Germany or Austria. The children of other countries involved in the war too had absent parents and were often orphaned. French and British families undoubtedly experienced the sense of fatherlessness and desertion by the mother as much as did German and Austrian families. Two added factors, however, make the critical difference in the constellation of the child's view of the world: the absence of German and Austrian parents was coupled with extreme and persistent hunger bordering in the cities on starvation, and when the German or Austrian father returned he came in defeat and was unable to protect his family in the postwar period of unemployment and inflation. Not only was the nation defeated, but the whole political-social world was overturned. The Kaiser of Germany had fled, and the Kaiser of Austria had been deposed. Some Germans would say that the Kaiser had deserted his people, to be replaced by an insecure and highly ambivalent republic under equivocating socialist leadership. Much more than an army collapsed—an entire orientation to the state and the conduct of civic life was under assault in 1918–19. These national factors unique to Central Europe exacerbated the familial crisis of the absence of parents and made of this wartime experience a generational crisis.

Today it is widely recognized that the emotional constellation of the childhood years is decisive for the future psychological health and normality of the adult. Modern war conditions, through the long-term breakup of family life, added in some cases to a lack of essential food and shelter, and a national atmosphere highly charged with unmitigated expressions of patriotism, hatred, and violence must inevitably distort the emotional and mental development of children, for imbalance in the fulfillment of essential psychic and bodily needs in childhood results in lasting psychological malformations. . . .

The most original psychoanalytical approach to National Socialist youth, and the one that I find conceptually most perceptive and useful, is Martin Wangh's excellent analysis of 1964. He structures the psychodynamics of the First World War German children who came to the age of political effectiveness with the rise of Hitler with precision and insight. A preoccupation with guilt, Wangh points out, is also an unrecognized self-reproach for unresolved aggression against the father. Aggression toward the absent father-rival is expressed in gleeful ideas concerning his degradation and defeat. But the hostility is coupled with a longing for the idealized father that exacerbates childish homosexual wishes. These homosexual longings offer a way out of the Oedipal conflict that is heightened for sons left alone with their mothers. In these circumstances the woman is often rejected, and the incestuous wish is ascribed to someone else. These mental defenses, Wangh suggests, were renewed in the Nazi movement's deification of the Führer and its infernalization of the Jew. Homosexual tension was relieved through submission to an all-powerful leader, through turning women into "breeders" of children, and by persecuting Jews as "incestuous criminals" and "defilers of the race." The passive-masochistic inclinations that develop when boys are brought up and disciplined by mothers who are anxious and punitive may be defended against by preference for submission to a man, as this is less threatening and less castrating than submission to a woman. Self-humiliation and self-contempt were displaced onto the Jews and other supposedly inferior people, thereby assuaging feelings of unworthiness and masochistic fantasies of rejection. Since the former wartime enemies were for the time being unassailable, the Jew, who was defenseless and available, became by the mechanism of displacement the victim of those who needed a target for regressive action.

This line of research has been carried on to the contemporary problem of the children of World War II. Herman Roskamp, in a clinical study of German university students born during the Second World War, emphasizes the conflict between the child's perception of the father during the war as a highly idealized fantasy object bearing his ideas of omnipotence and the way in which the father was perceived on his return in defeat. While away the father had been honored and admired; he was the object of extreme hopes and expectations upon his return. It quickly became apparent that he was not what had been longed for. Instead he was a defeated, insecure father breaking into a heretofore fatherless family. Up to this time the mother had represented all aspects of reality. The father, by contrast, was now a demanding rival who left most wishes unfulfilled, who disappointed many hopes, and who set many limits where formerly there had been none.

Among the richest sources for the expression of the experience of young Germans during the war and postwar years is the literature of the period, which more than held its place amid the cultural fecundity of the Weimar epoch. Sometimes literary expression can capture for historians the essence of a generation's experience both graphically and with a depth of emotional subtlety that cannot be conveyed by statistics or quantitative data. Many qualitative affects cannot be statistically comprehended or documented. It is possible to see, identify, and demonstrate father identification and castration anxiety without necessarily being able to computerize them. This is the appeal to the historian of both clinical insight and literary sensibility. Can one measure or compare quantitatively, for example, the degree of suffering, mourning, loss, or rage a subject feels? For this kind of emotional evidence we must rely on that most sensitive of our cultural materials—the subjective written word of literature.

When this has been said, it is nevertheless astonishing to experience the great autobiographical pacifist novel *Jahrgang 1902* by Ernst Glaeser (1902–63), which describes the author's feelings with

such intensity and pathos that it often reads more like the free associations of a patient in psychoanalysis than a novel. The critic William Soskin ranked *Jahrgang 1902* with *Sergeant Grisha* and *All
Quiet on the Western Front* as one of the most significant works on
the First World War. This book ran through six German printings during the winter of 1928–29. It sold seventy thousand copies in Germany and was translated into twenty-five languages.

The book takes its title from the year of the author's birth, which
also automatically became the year of his military service class. The
class of 1902 was not to experience the war of 1914–18 on the front.
For that they were too young, but as Glaeser pointedly noted, "The
war did not establish a moratorium on puberty." The book, he said,
deals with "the tragedy of murdered minds and souls and diseased
temperaments in the noncombatant social body."

As the war began the fathers left to join their regiments and the
twelve-year-old boy observes that "life in our town became quieter."
The boys played war games in which the French and Russians were
always soundly beaten. The fathers were sorely missed. They were
quickly idealized and glorified. Glaeser describes the process of
overestimation and identification with the father who is absent at
war:

> We thought only of our fathers in these days. Overnight they had become
> heroes. . . . We loved our fathers with a new sublime love. As ideals. And
> just as we formerly used to express our admiration for the Homeric heroes
> or the figures of the Wars of Liberation by token symbols of clothing such
> as golden helmets of tin foil or Lützow caps, so we now also began, but
> in far greater measure, to turn ourselves symbolically into the idealized
> figures of our fathers.

The boys of the village went to the barber to have their hair cut in
the close-cropped military style like their fathers.

> We had our hair cut. Bare. Smooth. Three millimeters high. For this is how
> we had seen it on our fathers as they left for the front. None of them had
> hair to part now.
>
> One evening late in September a group of fifteen determined boys
> went to the barber. We stood according to height and let the instrument
> pass over our heads. As the barber was sweeping up our hair with a
> broom an hour later, he said: "Now you look like recruits."
>
> We were proud of this distinction and enthusiastically paid forty pfen-
> nigs each.

By the winter of 1916 the privation of the war began to be felt in the daily lives of the boys. They were always hungry. There was never enough to eat. The steady diet of turnip soup became inedible. City folk bribed and bartered away precious possessions in order to get nourishing food from the farmers. The mother gave Kathinka, the maid, one of her finest blouses so that she would bring back food when she visited her peasant parents. Faithfully Kathinka smuggled butter past the gendarmes in her woolen bloomers. Field gendarmes and controllers appeared on the roads and at the stations to search travelers for contraband foodstuffs. The children developed tactics for deceiving the gendarmes and smuggling forbidden foodstuffs home. One boy would serve as a decoy to draw the gendarme's attention while the other raced home across the fields with a sack of flour or a ham.

This progression within two years from idealism to hunger and the struggle for survival is vividly described by Glaeser.

> *The winter remained hard until the end. The war began to burst over the fronts and to strike the people. Hunger destroyed our unity; in the families children stole each other's rations. . . . Soon the women who stood in gray lines in front of the shops talked more about the hunger of their children than of the death of their husbands. The sensations of war had been altered.*
>
> *A new front existed. It was held by women. The enemies were the entente of field gendarmes and uncompromising guards. Every smuggled pound of butter, every sack of potatoes gleefully secreted by night was celebrated in the families with the same enthusiasm as the victories of the armies two years earlier. . . . It was wonderful and inspiring to outwit the gendarmes and after successfully triumphing to be honored by one's mother as a hero.*

Oedipal longings were heightened for the sons left alone with their mothers during years of war. Starvation led to the mobilization of unconscious wishes for a return to the oral comforts of early mother-child units. Occasionally the prolonged hunger was broken by feasting on an illegally slaughtered pig or a smuggled goose that the father sent home from the eastern front. Then an orgy of feeding took place. Gluttony reigned and undernourished bellies got sick on the rich food. The windows had to be stuffed to keep the neighbors from smelling the meat. The adolescent boy and his mother consumed almost an entire twelve-pound goose in one night. A stolen drumstick for his girlfriend was to her the convincing symbol of love. Glaeser writes, "We scarcely spoke of the war any more, we only spoke of hunger. Our mothers were closer to us than our fathers."

The fathers were not present to shield the sons from maternal seduction. One young adolescent in the novel is seduced by a motherly farmer's wife with the promise of a large ham. But, much as the pangs of his stomach and his mother's pleading letters argued for bringing the ham home, he could not do it. The great succulent ham had become an incestuous object. He had earned it from the farm wife by taking her husband's place. Now he was too guilty and too anxious to permit himself and his family to enjoy it. The pangs of guilt were stronger than the pains of hunger. As if he could "undo" his Oedipal crime, the boy laid the ham on the farm wife's bed and left. He was tearful and depressed, feelings he rationalized as being due to his injured feelings because he was really only a substitute (*ersatz*) for the husband. He climbed into bed with his boy comrade. In the stillness of the dawn they embraced, keeping each other warm, and he shared his story of seduction and sexual discovery. In this episode we see fully elaborated the heightened Oedipal conflict when the father is absent, the increased guilt and fear of retribution, and finally the rejection of the woman as a sexual object and an exacerbation of adolescent homosexuality arising from the emotional effects of the war.

By the winter of 1917 the fathers had become aliens to their sons. But they were not only unknown men, they were feared and threatening strangers who claimed rights and control over the lives of their sons. They had become distant but powerful figures who could punish and exact a terrible price for disobedience and transgressions. Glaeser recounts his reaction as a fifteen-year-old to a letter from his father on the Russian front in terms of intense castration anxiety. The adolescent boy's Oedipal victory in having displaced his father would now be terribly expiated and revenged by a towering, castrating monster of his guilt-laden fantasies. Glaeser attempts to deny that his father has any legitimate claim to control over him at all. But his father would know where to find him and the inevitable retribution would be inexorable.

We were frightened. That was the voice of the front. That was the voice of those men who merely were once our fathers, who now, however, re-

moved from us for years, were strangers before us, fearsome, huge, over-powering, casting dark shadows, oppressive as a monument. What did they still know of us? They knew where we lived, but they no longer knew what we looked like and thought.

It is of biographical interest for the thesis of this essay that Glaeser went into emigration from Germany after 1933, living in Prague, Zurich, and Paris. In Zurich in 1939 he wrote a newspaper article condoning Hitler's policies and condemning his fellow emigrés. Within days he received a contract from a Berlin publisher. He returned to Germany and joined the war effort, becoming a war reporter for the Luftwaffe and the editor of the military newspaper, *Adler im Suden.*

Thus, as did so many others of his cohort, Glaeser was two decades later to choose to wear a uniform and to identify with his distant and glorified father. The identification with the father who went out to war served to erase the memory of the feared and hated strange father who came home in defeat. By being a patriot and submitting to authority, the ambivalence of the young boy who gleefully observed his father's humiliating defeat and degradation was denied and expiated. Now he would do obeisance to an idealized but remote leader who was deified and untouchable.

Many of the emotions of German middle-class generational conflict in the decade after World War I were profoundly explored by Thomas Mann in his story of 1925, "Disorder and Early Sorrow." The setting is the home of Professor Cornelius, a historian, the time is during the inflation of 1923, and the social climate is filled with anxiety about loss of status, a widening gap between the cultures of youth and adults, and the deepening economic crisis that has caused a deterioration of faith in stable moral norms. Solid bourgeois ladies are now the Corneliuses' house servants while the brash young man who lives by speculation, drives a car, treats his friends to champagne suppers, and showers the children of the professor with gauche gifts of "barbaric" size and taste represents the postwar generation.

The story opens with the menu of the midday meal in which the main dish is croquettes made of turnip greens. The meatless dinner is a meager contrast to the opulent menus succulently described by Mann in *Buddenbrooks* and *The Magic Mountain.* What reader can easily forget the sumptuous repasts in the restaurant of the International Sanitorium Berghof or Mann's descriptions of solid fare on the table of the patrician merchant home in the Hanseatic seaport? In the professorial home of the Weimar era the dessert is a powdered pudding that tastes of almonds and soap—an *ersatz* concoction symbolizing the current hard times and the decline in standard of living. Many people have had to give up their telephones, but the Corneliuses have so far been able to keep theirs. Repairs cannot be made on the house for lack of materials. The professor washes at a broken basin that cannot be repaired because there is nobody to mend it. Clothing is worn and turned, yet the adolescents of the family do not notice, for they wear a simple belted linen smock and sandals. They are, says Mann, by birth the "villa proletariat" [*Villenproletarier*] who no longer know or care about the correct evening dress of the middle classes or the manners of a gentleman. In fact, the professor cannot, from observing their style of dress or personal bearing, distinguish his son from his working-class Bolshevik household servant. "Both, he thinks, look like young moujiks." His children are products of the disrupted times, specimens of their generation, with a jargon of their own that the adults find incomprehensible. The young enjoy contriving to get the family extra allotments of rationed foods, such as eggs, by deceiving the shopkeepers. They function better than the old folk in a world in which money has lost its value. The generational struggle is underlined by the professor's consistent mental depreciation of his adolescent son when comparing him with other young men: "And here is my poor Bert, who knows nothing and can do nothing and thinks of nothing except playing the clown, without even talent for that!" The younger son, who is but four years old, is subject to the rages of "a howling dervish." He, who is "born and brought up in these desolate, distracted times, ... has been endowed by them with an unstable and hypersensitive nervous system and suffers greatly under life's disharmonies. He is prone to sudden anger and outbursts of bitter tears, stamping his feet at every trifle."

Thus Mann pictures the dislocation of continuity between the generations of the Weimar republic. They differ in expectations and methods of dealing with reality. In the decade since 1913, when the professor bought his home, the family has in fact been proletarianized. One of the themes of the story is their varied response, as individuals of different ages, to this fact. The old generation cannot adjust, while their children are born into the new situation and need not make any adaptation of life style. Mann has sketched superbly and for all time the psychological experience of the impoverishment of the German upper-middle class and the rebellion against the norms and values of their parents by the children of the war.

The third variety of data I wish to examine is quantitative. It is a series of autobiographical essays collected in 1934 by Theodore Abel, a sociologist at Columbia University, in an essay contest offering cash prizes for "the best personal life history of an adherent of the Hitler movement. . . ."

The most striking emotional affect expressed in the Abel autobiographies are the adult memories of intense hunger and privation from childhood. A party member who was a child of the war years recollects, "Sometimes I had to scurry around eight to ten hours—occasionally at night—to procure a few potatoes or a bit of butter. Carrots and beets, previously considered fit only for cattle, came to be table luxuries." Another man's memory is vivid in its sense of abandonment and isolation expressed in language that makes a feeling of maternal deprivation very clear.

> Hunger was upon us. Bread and potatoes were scarce, while meat and fats were almost nonexistent. We were hungry all the time; we had forgotten how it felt to have our stomachs full.
>
> All family life was at an end. None of us really knew what it meant—we were left to our own devices. For women had to take the place of their fighting men. They toiled in factories and in offices, as ostlers and as commercial travelers, in all fields of activity previously allotted to men—behind the plow as well as on the omnibus. Thus while we never saw our fathers, we had only glimpses of our mothers in the evening. Even then they could not devote themselves to us because, tired as they were, they had to take care of their household, after their strenuous day at work. So we grew up, amid hunger and privation, with no semblance of decent family life.

A study of the Abel autobiographies focused on a sample from the birth cohorts 1911 to 1915, who were small children during the war, indicates the presence of the defensive mechanisms of projection, displacement, low frustration tolerance, and the search for an idealized father. For example, the essays of two sisters born in 1913 and 1915, whose father fell in 1915, clearly demonstrate that Hitler served as an idealized father figure for them. Their earliest memories are of their mother crying a great deal and of all the people wearing black. They relate their excitement at first hearing the Führer speak in person at a rally in Kassel in 1931. The sisters were so exhilarated that neither of them could sleep all night. They prayed for the protection of the Führer, and asked forgiveness for ever having doubted him. The sisters began their Nazi party activities by caring for and feeding SA men. . . .

The demographic factors of massive health, nutritional, and material deprivation and parental absence in Central Europe during World War I should lead the historian to apply theoretical and clinical knowledge of the long-term effects of such a deprived childhood on personality. The anticipation of weakened character structure manifested in aggression, defenses of projection and displacement, and inner rage that may be mobilized by a renewed anxiety-inducing trauma in adulthood is validated in the subsequent political conduct of this cohort during the Great Depression when they joined extremist paramilitary and youth organizations and political parties. In view of these two bodies of data for which a psychoanalytic understanding of personality provides the essential linkage, it is postulated that a direct relationship existed between the deprivation German children experienced in World War I and the response of these children and adolescents to the anxieties aroused by the Great Depression of the early 1930s. This relationship is psychodynamic: the war generation had weakened egos and superegos, meaning that the members of this generation turned readily to programs based on facile solutions and violence when they met new frustrations during the depression. They then reverted to earlier phase-specific fixations in their child development marked by rage, sadism, and the defensive idealization of their absent parents, especially the father. These elements made this age cohort particularly susceptible to the appeal of a mass movement utilizing the crudest devices of projection and displacement in its ideology. Above all it prepared the young voters of Germany for submission to a total, charismatic leader.

But fantasy is always in the end less satisfying than mundane reality. Ironically, instead of finding the idealized father they, with Hitler as their leader, plunged Germany and Europe headlong into a series of deprivations many times worse than those of World War I. Thus the repetition was to seek the glory of identification with the absent soldier-father, but like all quests for a fantasied past, it had to fail.

Hitler and National Socialism were so much a repetition and fulfillment of the traumatic childhoods of the generation of World War I that the attempt to undo that war and those childhoods was to become a political program. As a result the regressive illusion of nazism ended in a repetition of misery at the front and starvation at home made worse by destroyed cities, irremediable guilt, and millions of new orphans.

A return to the past is always unreal. To attempt it is the path of certain disaster. There was no glorified father who went to war and who could be recaptured in Hitler. He existed only in fantasy, and he could never be brought back in reality. There are no ideal mothers and fathers; there are only flawed human parents. Therefore, for a World War I generation seeking restitution of a lost childhood there was to be only bitter reality in the form of a psychotic charlatan who skillfully manipulated human needs and left destruction to Germany and Europe. What the youth cohort wanted was a fantasy of warmth, closeness, security, power, and love. What they re-created was a repetition of their own childhoods. They gave to their children and to Europe in greater measure precisely the traumas they had suffered as children and adolescents a quarter of a century earlier.

Mihaly Samson
Laszlo Beke

STREET PEOPLE SPEAK: THE HUNGARIAN REVOLT

Mihaly Samson and "Laszlo Beke"—a pseudonym—were actual participants in the Hungarian revolt against Russian domination in 1956. Both were student demonstrators; Beke was one of the organizers of the Student Revolutionary Council itself. The following extracts are from their respective diaries for October of that year: Samson's journal is extracted at length in Tibor Meray's That Day in Budapest: October 23, 1956 *(1969); Beke's is reprinted from his own book,* A Student's Diary: Budapest, October 16–November 1, 1956 *(1957). These two first-hand accounts, taken together, reveal more vividly than any structural analysis the peculiarly powerful momentum of the Youth Revolution once launched into action in the streets.*

The Hungarian insurrection of 1956, so powerfully depicted in these two diaries, was the first large-scale revolt against the Russian hegemony that had been clamped on East Europe in the wake of World War II. The same fierce nationalism that had led Hungarians to rebel against Habsburg Austria in 1848 had led them to resent bitterly the "satellite" status imposed on them by the Russians in 1945. In the fall of 1956, this resentment flared into open revolt—a rebellion spearheaded, as so often in the past, by the militant youth.

FROM MIHALY SAMSON'S DIARY

It is three o'clock in the morning. What date, exactly, should I put at the head of these notes: the twenty-second or the twenty-third? If I stick to the course of the events that I am describing, it is October 22; if I consider the time of writing (after midnight), it is October 23.... What frivolity to dally over such petty details! Always that same mania of the engineer-to-be: precision and exactitude at all costs.... Granted, the sensible thing to do would be to go to sleep; meeting at ten tomorrow morning, everyone at school.... My head is spinning, overloaded with everything that I was able to watch and listen to since yesterday afternoon. Go to sleep? Suppose my impressions blur overnight? Suppose I forget or distort? Again the damned obsession of mathematical precision....

Unless the impulse that drives me to get everything down on paper is set off by something else? In other circumstances the word *historic,* so pompous and debased, would have discouraged me; now, on the contrary, that adjective has an impact on me that is stimulating. I feel compelled to use it for the first time in my life. Yes, I must write out these notes on this *historic day....*

Monday, after lunch: that was when everything started ... October 22, 1956, at three o'clock in the afternoon.

Big meeting at the university with the participation of the professors, the party leaders, and the heads of the Youth Movement. We were about five thousand! An unforgettable meeting that lasted eleven hours without a break, all of us talking all the time—we

Hungarians are so good at that. This time, however, it was not a business of empty words. First of all there was the question of purely university demands: lower fares on public transportation, reductions in textbook prices, improvements in students' housing, etc. Little by little the problems that we were discussing became increasingly interesting: there were protests against the length of the courses in Marxism and the emphasis placed on them in the program; some said they wanted to be able to choose courses in other languages than Russian: English, French, German. When evening came we got down to more important questions. One of us got up to give a brief report on recent events in Poland. According to him, and I think he is right, Comrade Gomulka wanted his country to develop in a natural, peaceful way according to the laws of democracy. Our colleague emphasized the solid foundation of this program. Unfortunately, he said, its backers had to confront the opposition of the Soviet Union when Khrushchev, Kaganovitch, Mikoyan, and Molotov unexpectedly arrived to take part in the meeting of the Polish party's Central Committee while units of the Soviet army encircled the capital. And yet, he said, the good cause triumphed! In spite of all these efforts Gomulka was elected first secretary of the Polish party and did not conceal from the Soviet leaders the fact that he was completely informed of their army's maneuvers to surround the capital; the Polish army, he said, was prepared to reply with force if there were any incidents. Our colleague told us the source of this information: a Russian-language broadcast from a Polish station. His talk set off indiscribable enthusiasm. Everyone began to shout: "Long live Gomulka! Long live our Polish sister nation! Democracy in Hungary!"

Another student, in his fourth year in architecture, got up and asked for the floor to present an analysis of the situation that in my opinion was perfect.

"In the Soviet Union," he said, "the leadership has embarked on the liquidation of the Stalinist inheritance. Eight months ago, during the Twentieth Congress of the Soviet party, Comrade Khrushchev revealed Stalin's crimes. The disclosure was followed by all kinds of reforms in the Soviet Union: in agriculture, industry, legislation, party organization. I do not deny the progress that has been made among us; during the eighteen months when Imre Nagy was

premier things advanced considerably in Hungary.[1] We breathed
more freely. But Rakosi turned Nagy out of office in order to push
us back into a 'second Stalinism.' In July of this year we finally got
rid of Rakosi. We are not unaware of the part played by our Soviet
comrades in the expulsion of 'our little Stalin.' We are grateful to
them for it. At that time we hoped for a quick improvement in our
position. Nothing of the kind followed. Here we are at the end of
October without having seen any true reform, any democratic
change; things are still being dragged out indefinitely. The present
leaders still seem to be dominated by the shadows of Rakosi and
Stalin. See how the Polish comrades take their country's destiny
into their own hands! ... Once the surprise and apprehension of the
beginning have vanished, the Soviet comrades themselves will
approve them in the end. Why shouldn't we Hungarians follow their
example? Why shouldn't we profit now by the changes that have
taken place in Poland?"

"Long live Imre Nagy!" someone interrupted. "Long live the Hungarian Gomulka!"

"Exactly, long live Imre Nagy, and may he return to the leadership of the country," the architectural student said. Then he went
on: "But it's not just a question of changing personnel; we need a
new program. An over-all program, but one that points new roads
for us, with precision. It's up to us to state the major demands of
our nation. Just like 108 years ago, we are charged with defining
what the Hungarian nation demands."

A thrill of excitement ran through the whole audience. The great
events of 1848 had begun 108 years ago in Budapest in a place very
near this one, thanks to the work of the youth in revolt, which, two
generations before our own, had laid down twelve points of *The
Demands of the Hungarian Nation.* How intoxicating this analogy
was for us, who perhaps are the bearers of the same historic mission. ... There were shouts: "The nation's demands! ... Come on,
let's put them into writing! ... Right! Everyone down to work, right
away!"

The whole crowd was swept up in the general enthusiasm. Twenty

---

[1] Imre Nagy has been made premier once before October 1956: in June 1953, through
the vigorous intervention of the Kremlin. Denounced as a "right-wing deviationist"
not eighteen but twenty months later, in April 1955 he was stripped of his post.—
Author.

or thirty hands went up from people who wanted to propose demands: freedom of speech, freedom of action, freedom of the press, democratic elections, to mention just a few of them.

Soon other demands came to light, all of them probably natural; but they could not be formulated without prior discussion. A student near me said: "This would be the time to demand that Soviet troops get out of Hungary. We must put that demand into our program."

We disagreed with him. "No, it's not for you to make such a proposal," someone said.

"For whom, then?"

"Someone who is trusted. A party official, for example."

Then the assistant secretary of the Young Communists got up and went to the microphone: "Dear comrades and colleagues," he said, "we can easily draft demands, but, as long as the Soviet army retains its power over us, we will not gain any modification in the direction of political affairs."

Then other speakers attacked our election procedures, which are so different from those of free elections. . . . Still others demanded freedom of expression and religion and travel. All together we evolved a draft resolution. It was decided to take it to the radio station in order to have it included in the evening news broadcast.

It was eight-thirty when our delegation reached the station. I was in it, with three fellows from my school. We were allowed to enter under the surveillance of a guard who accompanied us to the office of the editor in chief of news broadcasts, a tired, blonde little man who looked understanding. After he had run quickly through the text that we had prepared, he seemed to be making excuses: "You know as well as I do, my young friends, that we cannot broadcast such demands on Radio Budapest's air."

"Is what we have said so terrible, then?"

The editor sighed, wiped his forehead, and called one of his associates: "Here, take this resolution and write a short bulletin with these young comrades about the meeting that they had this afternoon. . . . Above all, nothing derogatory. Let me have your copy in ten minutes."

Barely three-quarters of an hour later we heard for ourselves the "little not derogatory bulletin" on the radio. It spoke briefly of a meeting at the university at three o'clock in the afternoon. The announcer hastily mentioned "student demands" and added: "Certain provocations were noted but the majority of the young audience would have nothing to do with them."

We are quite familiar with the system of political fakery. Discouraged, we left the station and started back to our meeting. It was noisy enough before we got there, but, when we had reported on our mission, it turned even more feverish. "More censorship!" someone shouted.

Finally we received unexpected help from an editor of *Szabad Ifjusag (Free Youth)*, the Young Communists' newspaper. He was given the floor and he said that he approved of our demands and was prepared to have them printed in his paper; but he advised us to delete the passage dealing with the withdrawal of Soviet troops. "Publishing that would have a disastrous effect," he said.

The reaction of disapproval was unanimous: "We refuse any censorship. We'd rather find a way on our own."

Five students went off, with a copy of the resolution, to have it placed in the university's newspaper, which prints two thousand copies. One of us rose and addressed the rector of the university: "Comrade Rector, the university has duplicating machines for text materials. Give us permission to use them to circulate our demands."

The rector took refuge in an evasive answer: "You're excited. . . . You are not cautious enough. . . . You must be patient. . . . I no longer agree with you. . . ." He is an old man who cannot keep up with the young. So we set up a little clandestine group, and, while the rector was still acting as chairman of this endless meeting, we went off and in a few hours we had produced several thousand copies of our demands.

Meanwhile the meeting decided that a "Youth Parliament" would be convened on the twenty-seventh to discuss the various points in the resolution. The debate will be of national importance. We are inviting the Hungarian radio to record it and broadcast it so that the whole world can hear the voice of Hungarian youth.

During the evening discussion Zoltan Zelk, representing the Association of Hungarian Writers, asked for the floor. We all know him by name and we were happy to have him there. But his speech left us dissatisfied: He announced that on the twenty-third the writers intend to stage a small commemorative ceremony near the statue of General Joseph Bem, a Hungarian and Polish national hero of the revolutions of 1848, and that a wreath would be placed at the foot of the statue and there would be a short speech, but that the writers were planning no demonstrations.

We were disappointed, and we immediately decided that the students of the Technical University would organize one. Our professors began to speak: "Above all be careful!"

But we will be! All we want is a silent, calm, peaceful demonstration. That is the only thing that can make it possible for us to attain our goal!... (That is not merely my opinion, everyone else holds the same view.)

Our meeting ended at two o'clock in the morning. We left the university, but we could not resign ourselves to separating, and so we kept on talking in the street in a number of lively small groups. Soon it was three o'clock; we had walked to the dormitory, taking an hour to cover the few hundred yards from the university....

Now it is five twenty-three. I was about to mention the seconds as well.... To bed, young man! You have to be in shape for the ten o'clock appointment at school; it looks like a busy, exciting day....

FROM LASZLO BEKE'S DIARY

The first important news today was the refusal of the government to grant our request for a ceremony at the square. The refusal was broadcast on the early morning newscast.

Then the council turned to me with a near-impossible task: to prepare quickly a leaflet that could be printed that morning and distributed to approximately twenty thousand people. The fourteen points were to be the basis of the message.

And if anyone thinks it is an easy job to find that much paper, and a place to print, in a Communist-held country, I can assure you it isn't. But I managed to get my hands on Communist-issued stationery and a university rubber stamp. With this I forged a document which gained access for us to the room that housed the small university printing press.

From *A Student's Diary: Budapest, October 16–November 1, 1956* by Laszlo Beke, pp. 25–36; Leon Kossar and Ralph M. Zoltan, editors and translators. Copyright © 1957 by Laszlo Beke. Reprinted by permission of The Viking Press, Inc. and The Macmillan Company of Canada Limited.

Within two hours' time we were running off leaflets.

At 2:30 p.m., twelve thousand students and youths had gathered at Petofi Square near the Danube River. At precisely this hour we renamed our organization the Students' Revolutionary Council— using the word "Revolutionary" for the first time. But at this time no one imagined a revolution of blood equaling the French Revolution in fury of battle, dedication to ideal, and sacrifices on the altar of freedom.

Every window was open, and Hungarian flags appeared as if by magic. Some of the flags had the Red Star in the center cut out and removed. Other people saw these and followed the example on their own flags.

We wanted to act in sympathy with the students who had led the Poznan riots, and to stress the long friendship between Poland and Hungary. We chose Jozsef Bem Square as our demonstration site, for Bem was a Polish hero and one of the military leaders in Hungary's 1848 revolution against Austria.

Bem Square was at least two and a half miles away from Petofi Square. We had to march through almost the entire downtown section of Pest.

The march started out quietly along Kossuth Lajos Street. It seemed that everyone in the city knew about it even before it began. People stepped out of doorways to join the march, or left their homes and jobs to catch up with us at street corners. Many of the students carried flags, while others distributed leaflets along the way. Flags appeared all along the route we took. Traffic stopped completely, and government stores and offices closed as employees rushed outside to see what was happening.

We started out with twelve thousand—but our parade grew longer and longer as we moved along Bajcsy-Zsilinsky Street, Marx Square, and St. Stephen Boulevard. By the time we reached St. Margaret Bridge there were anywhere from fifty thousand to eighty thousand people with us.

There was no parade marshal, and no schedule for what the huge crowd was to do next.

As we marched by the Ministry of Culture and Education building, I spied one of the top Communist officials of the University Section watching the parade from the gate. I pulled another student after me, and we ran over to the startled official. I took one arm, my fellow marcher the other, and we dragged Comrade Palasti into the student procession.

We grinned at him and shouted, "Down with Gero! Down with Rakosi!" (Gero was the Moscow stooge who was first secretary of the Communist Central Committee. Rakosi was his predecessor as Communist boss of Hungary.) Our captive managed a sick grin back, although he was thoroughly frightened.

Even women with small babies in their arms joined our march. Bem Square filled slowly with more than a hundred thousand people. It was a heaving, restless throng.

It was about 4 p.m.

Here and there in the packed square student shouts were taken up by the crowd. "Out with the Russians! . . . Down with Rakosi! . . . We won't be slaves any longer! . . .

"New flags . . . new government . . . freedom of speech . . ." The words echoed off the buildings.

As I stood in the street square a voice from underneath the statue called itself hoarse without the aid of loudspeakers:

> *"Magyars, rise! Your country calls!*
> *Meet this hour, whate'er befalls!*
> *Shall we freemen be, or slaves?*
> *Choose the lot your spirit craves!"*

The words of the Petofi poem gripped the demonstrators nearby.

As tension mounted, Budapest's Communist radio reported that masses of students were demonstrating in the streets and that there were "Fascist rumors that Hungary wants to loosen its ties with the friendly Soviet Union."

From several scores of loudspeakers placed in windows and doorways of Bem Square the hated voice of Gero, a man only the AVH secret police would trust, broadcast this lie of lies: "The Communists are Hungarian patriots." We shouted back, "Down with Gero! . . . We want freedom!"

Right behind us, facing the Danube River, just off Bem Square, were the Radetzky Barracks. There were only one or two battalions stationed there. The heavy gates stood closed, and the guards had left their posts some time ago to mix with our crowd.

Suddenly the gates swung open and soldiers streamed out, cheering and waving. They had torn the Red Star off their military caps. They came out to join us without weapons, for no one knew how badly we would need arms in the next few hours.

Darkness was already setting in when we left Bem Square and split into two groups. The smaller of the two student groups made for Dozsa Gyorgy Boulevard, where Budapest citizens were already tugging at the huge twenty-five-foot Stalin monument. It wasn't too long before this hated symbol of Bolshevism crumbled. Three of the students had helped put a rope around Stalin's neck, and minutes later he stumbled from his perch on broken knees after the rioting crowd had pulled him bodily off his pedestal of honor.

The larger student group, the one I helped to muster, headed for the parliament buildings—a distance of about a mile from Bem Square, on the Pest side.

The thousands who marched with us over St. Margaret Bridge to Balaton Street were already past the boiling point.

We passed the headquarters of the hated AVH police. The doors were locked, the blinds were down. The building looked quite abandoned, and we couldn't see any of the people who were first on our hate list.

We thought of the thousands and thousands of good patriots who had been tortured and murdered in this building. We shouted and whistled and waved our fists as we passed by. But the secret police seemed so far away at the moment it was as if we were shaking our fists at the sun for burning too brightly.

Evidence of the anger that had welled up within the Budapest citizens was all around us as we marched. One old fellow appeared at the door of his home with a picture of Rakosi in his hand. I saw him set fire to it and wave it at the cheering students who passed.

We plodded through hundreds of thousands of Communist and Marxist books, countless brochures, and pictures of Kremlin leaders and Hungarian puppets. We trampled the whole Communist way of life underfoot as we walked proudly and defiantly toward the parliament buildings. It was a gesture of hatred by the Hungarian people, as if they were preparing the people behind the pictures for us to walk over next.

On the way some youthful Hungarians ran out to tell us that Gero was preparing a threatening speech against the demonstrators, and would broadcast on Budapest Radio. Soon we were assembled in Parliament Square.

There was only one person we could think of who wasn't in prison at the time—one person we might possibly trust.

His name was Imre Nagy.

Because of his liberalism and his Titoist tendencies, Nagy had earlier been deposed as premier by Rakosi. It wasn't that he was the best leader to take over at that point; it was just that he was probably the only one who was alive. Others had been either shot or deported to Siberia.

The cry at the parliament buildings was "We want Nagy!" And every Hungarian heart was on fire as the words of the national anthem, "God Bless the Magyars," rose to a melodic fury above the crowd. "We want Nagy! Let's see Nagy!" The short phrases hammered at the ears of Communist officials behind locked doors.

But a half-hour went by and there was still no sign of Nagy.

A stout little man appeared twice on the balcony and promised, "Comrade Nagy will soon be here. Please be patient." We knew he was just trying to gain time.

"We don't want *Comrade* Nagy," we shouted. "We want *Mr.* Nagy, and we want him NOW!"

The Communists' answer was typical. They turned out all the lights in Parliament Square and left a hundred thousand people in a complete blackout.

This sort of answer made the crowd more furious. Everyone began to search pockets for pieces of paper, and in a few minutes thousands of little torches were lit, burning brightly for a few seconds, then disappearing to give way to others. The crowd began to sing the national anthem for the sixth time, and the voices got stronger and stronger. "Open the gates!" some began to cry. Soon the cry gave way to "We're going in!"

At last Imre Nagy arrived, summoned by frightened Communist officials. It was 10 p.m.

They brought him out to address the crowd. The square was still pitch dark, for the tiny flares were the only light, and we couldn't quite be sure it was he. The huge sea of people called for a spotlight on his face so they would be able to recognize the onetime premier.

Nagy began to speak, calmly and slowly. He asked the crowd

to disperse, and advised everyone to go home. But those of us in the front row noticed something strange as he spoke. During his speech Nagy bent backward several times, and at one point we distinctly heard a voice behind him say, "Stick to your paper." Those of us who heard the background prodding shouted out, "Leave Nagy alone up there on the balcony!" But they answered us simply by taking Nagy in from the balcony.

We saw that the glass was full now. We had to do something, and do it then. There was no power on earth to hold this seething mass of people back after this demonstration. We were prepared to try anything to transfer government authority to Nagy's hands.

But it became evident that students alone could not get far against the armed might of fifteen thousand secret police and the Soviet juggernaut that stood behind them.

We had to have the workers and the peasants behind us. They would have to stand with us as they did in 1919, when Hungary crushed communism the first time, proving that this country of nine million people was opposed to any kind of foreign domination. The first thing we had to do was get Radio Budapest in our hands. And we had to have our manifesto broadcast so that the whole nation would know exactly what was at stake.

We marched on the radio building.

The streets were littered with the debris of smashed windows, pictures, Communist material, as demonstrations became more and more violent following Gero's menacing words an hour ago. Thousands of men, women, and youths had joined the marching throng, and the whole thing turned into an eerie, paper-lit procession.

The Students' Revolutionary Council appointed Jeno Fay and Istvan Antal as the students who would represent us at the radio station and would seek to have our fourteen-point manifesto read. Sandor Street was on fire with excitement. Everyone felt that a turning point had definitely arrived. We knew if we could get the radio into our hands we could fire the whole populace of Hungary with our wonderful idea. The radio was our strongest weapon at this time. Twenty-five representatives of the demonstrators, students and workers went into the radio building with the two student spokesmen.

But the Communists realized our mission only too well. They were prepared for us. There were secret police troops everywhere we looked, and others on rooftops behind the ugly snouts of machine guns.

"Open up!" the crowd shouted.

Suddenly the gate opened, and seconds later a Red Cross car crashed through the yard. Near the front, we were able to see who the sick man was. Comrade Erno Gero, the cowardly Moscow marionette, used this trick to escape the wrath of the people.

We began to worry about our friends who had gone inside to make our demands known. They were to have been out in ten minutes. Half an hour passed, then a full hour. People began to beat on the heavy gates with their bare fists. "We want our students! We want our brothers!" they chorused.

The police state had lost all vestiges of authority by this time. No one would believe anything the Communists told him after this point. No one wanted to listen to lies any longer.

Then, all of a sudden, the bloodless revolution ended and a revolution of blood began. The signal for revolt was the ghastly sight of friends and relatives dying.

The heavy oaken gates of the radio building swung open like a gaping, hungry giant's mouth, and machine guns within the courtyard began rattling out a message of death. They spat death at defenseless men, women, and children. This was the first massacre in the October Revolt.

Just a few feet away from me the first victim of AVH machine gun bullets fell quietly to the ground, lifeless. I'll remember his name as our first sacrifice: Lieutenant Colonel Istvan Zeleczky of the Hungarian army. The Communist minister of the interior, Laszlo Piros, had ordered his killers to mow us down.

Seconds later, two close friends fell—our first university-student casualties. They were Geza Julis and Jeno Borhy.

Madness and confusion began to reign all around me. Everyone wanted to strike back. But we had no arms.

Four of us—Imre, Peti, Geze, and I—ran into the side street by the radio building to look for weapons. Around the corner there was a construction job in progress, and the first thing we saw was bricks —strong, heavy bricks.

We piled bricks on small carts used to move around mortar, and wheeled them back as fast as we could to the front of the radio building. When we got back we heard that our friends who had carried the petition in had also been slain by the AVH.

As soon as the others saw our bricks they took the same route and carried back load after load of bricks. Soon thousands of bricks were piled up before the gates, and everyone waited for a chance to begin the attack.

The gates opened briefly to let two women employees out. Behind them we saw two AVH men with machine guns. A whistle gave the signal, and hundreds of students and youths began pelting them with a brick hailstorm. Hit by several bricks, they began to stumble away from the guns to look for shelter. Two brave youths jumped forward to take their places at the guns. These were the first weapons we got. The young men aimed the machine guns at the inside door of the radio station. And as the rest of us fought with bare hands, hundreds of students were on their way to look for other arms.

My friend Peti Lorenc led a group that went to Csepel, the largest ammunition factory in Hungary, on the outskirts of Budapest. Others ran to a military barracks nearby. I took about fifty students of Jozsef Nador Technical University, and rushed to the City Police headquarters in Vigyazo Ferenc Street. This building was about two and one-half miles from Sandor Street and the radio building.

Two armed guards were at the gates. We brushed them aside when we saw mute approval on their faces. Feri Kovacs pinned tricolored ribbons on them as we went by. We broke in on the command room, where they kept round-the-clock watches.

"In the name of the Students' Revolutionary Council, surrender your arms!" I said, surprised at my own loud tones and wondering what the exact reaction would be.

The officer in charge, who had about two hundred policemen in the building at his beck and call, reminded me of one of my college professors as he studied my face. My heart pounded as I gazed at him, then at my student friends around me. We were defenseless. The next move was up to him.

Then the forty-five-year-old police major stepped up toward us and saluted me, a young man of twenty-five. "All right, boys," he said with a weak smile. I couldn't help rushing up to him and embracing him. He stood back with other police as we piled tommy guns, automatic weapons, hand grenades, and other arms on two trucks parked in the yard.

As many as could clambered aboard the trucks. We screamed back to the radio building. Sandor Street had already become a battleground.

There was no leader, no battle plan—except for the single purpose in everyone's mind, to capture the Radio Budapest building.

Barbara and John Ehrenreich

A RADICAL ANALYSIS: THE MAY DAYS IN PARIS

Barbara (b. 1941) and John (b. 1943) Ehrenreich, like Bolton King, have been social activists in their own country as well as observers of revolutionary activities abroad. This chapter from Long March, Short Spring *(1969) is an excellent example of the merging of first-hand observation with thoughtful radical analysis. In particular, the essay gives due weight to the issues, the stated grievances of the youthful revolutionaries—an aspect of generational revolt too often ignored by social scientists eager to get at the deeper causes of the youth revolution.*

The Ehrenreichs, both graduate students that violent spring of 1968, set out to tour Europe, observing and infusing what they saw with their own radical vision—a vision which, like Treitschke's nationalism, gave them a special empathy with the young revolutionaries they interviewed.

The May Days in Paris were only the latest in a long history of Paris "days" of rebellion against the status quo. Sometimes the rebels have swept to victory, as in the July Days of 1830. Sometimes they have died futilely on the barricades, like the ragged workers of the June 1848 revolt. But always, there has been a special flair, a surge of excitement about Paris insurrections that no others can match. The youth who took to the streets against President de Gaulle's geriatric authoritarianism lost the battle of the Latin Quarter. But they brought nearly a million Frenchmen into the streets in their

From Barbara and John Ehrenreich, *Long March, Short Spring: The Student Uprising at Home and Abroad* (New York: Monthly Review Press, 1969), pp. 73–89, 91–93, 97–99. Copyright © 1969 by Barbara and John Ehrenreich. Reprinted by permission of the Monthly Review Press.

support, triggered a paralyzing general strike by millions of French workers,
and undoubtedly contributed to de Gaulle's abrupt retirement from power
less than a year later.

The high point of the student movements of all the countries of
Europe in the spring of 1968 was, of course, May in France. The
student movement in France had mushroomed in the spring of 1968,
leading to violent clashes with the police. In sympathy, the national
confederations of trade unions called a one day general strike and
a giant demonstration. But the workers had grievances, too, and
once their energies were unleashed, they could not be imprisoned.
Factory after factory was occupied by its workers, until, by late May,
10 million workers were on strike. Tens of thousand of students
and workers marched through Paris, demanding "workers' power,
peasants' power, and students' power," waving red flags, and sing-
ing the *Internationale.* The revolutionary wave swept over people in
provincial towns too. At Nantes, the entire town was run as a commune by the workers.

The threat of revolution had come out of the jungles of Southeast
Asia and down from the highlands of Latin America. For the first
time in decades, an advanced capitalist state tottered on the edge.

The student movement which touched off the tumultuous events
of May was a young movement. There is no organization whose
history we can trace, as we can trace the story of German SDS,
through slow preparatory years. Nevertheless, the roots of the French
student revolt are much the same as in other European countries.
As elsewhere, Vietnam and the crisis of the educational system were
the initial causes for agitation. The difference between France and
the other European countries is that in France the working class
was becoming more militant on its own, so that when the students
lit the spark, the workers' movement caught fire. This, in turn, entirely transformed the student movement. Instead of following a
course like other young student movements which were born in the
fall of 1967 (such as the Italian movement), it leaped far beyond
the confines of the university, and completely changed our perceptions of the nature, role, and possibilities of students as revolutionaries.

An intensely politicized student population is nothing new to
France. During the Algerian War, thousands of French students

risked their careers and sometimes their lives to oppose French imperialism. With the end of the war and the rise of de Gaulle, activity waned, and most students went back to their books. De Gaulle's immense popularity seemed to leave no opening for attack. Besides, domestic issues were much more subtle than an imperialist war. It wasn't until 1965–66 that students found a clear focus for political activity again: the American war in Vietnam. A shadow of the urgency of the Algerian years returned, and many hundreds again became active. For the first time in years there was an issue which could rally apolitical and liberal students, as well as the ideologically committed. In a sense, Vietnam was an easy evasion of domestic issues. Even de Gaulle was against the war. But at the same time, Vietnam provided a hothouse atmosphere for budding militants. In opposing the war, you could talk and even act militantly without ever confronting the power of the state or of established Left organizations such as the giant Communist party.

What turned this militance into a mass movement, however, was the growing crisis in the universities. As in other European countries, university enrollment accelerated wildly in the 1960s. From 1960 to 1964 alone, the number of students attending the university grew by 60 percent. Then from 1965–68, the postwar baby boom added to this mushrooming student body. At the same time, the patterns of use of the university were shifting to meet the changing industrial demands. Enrollment in the Medical and Law Faculties dropped, relatively, as students shifted into the Faculties of Letters and of Sciences. The experience of attending the overcrowded universities became ever more alienating. As in Italy, professors read from their own textbooks to gigantic lecture classes. And large though the classes seemed, they contained only the small fraction of enrolled students who could fit into the classroom. The rest didn't even try; they bought a copy of the professor's lectures and read them at home.

Faced with a university which was meeting neither the needs of business for highly educated workers nor the needs of the students for a decent education, the government, like governments throughout Europe, had to initiate reforms of some kind. All of the reforms aimed at making the educational process speedier and more efficient. Up to now, everyone who passed his baccalaureate exam at the end of high school was automatically admitted to the university.

Once in, many students dragged out their stay almost indefinitely by working part time. One of the planned reforms would superimpose further selection procedures on the "bac" and then eliminate part-time study for the lucky entrants. The curriculum reforms, proposed in 1963 by Fouchet, then minister of education, would channel entering students into one of several specialized paths: one would lead to academic research, another to narrow, nontheoretical training as a technician, another to teaching. Training in liberal arts and training in sciences would be neatly separated—if possible, in separate buildings.

Thus, the old wholesale wine market in Paris was demolished to make way for the new Faculty of Science, at a safe distance from the Faculties of Letters and Philosophy. Far out on the outskirts of Paris, near a train station appropriately named La Folie ("madness"), a new Faculty of Letters rose from the fields of Nanterre. But new buildings cannot update curriculum and teaching methods. The transplanted students found they had the same old grievances, plus the added problem of geographical isolation. Nanterre is situated in what can only be described as a very large field of mud.

If the old university had been oppressive, the "reformed" one would be intolerable. One of the early complaints about the Fouchet Plan was not, however, its content, but that students had never been consulted in drafting it. From this first notion of their own right to make "the decisions that affect their lives," the next question was obvious for the students: who *did* make the decisions? The Ministry of Education, the national government. And from there, why did they make *this* decision? In the interests of business and government, certainly not for the students' sake. Then the final question was: why should our education, in fact our careers, serve *them,* anyway? Students asked the same questions all over France. At Nanterre and at the Sorbonne, at Strasbourg and at Nantes, student protest movements sprang up in the spring and fall of 1967.

In France, discontent escalated very rapidly to articulate protest. For one thing, the French educational system, like almost everything else French, is highly centralized. It is the minister of education, not the professors or the rector of a university, who has the power to initiate reforms. When agitation erupted into action, local authorities were powerless to meet it with even minor adjustments. The whole affair got dumped on the steps of the Ministry of Education. For the students, conflict with the university meant conflict with the state.

At this point, many of the students were on familiar ground. Marxism is ingrained in French student culture much the way liberalism is a part of American student culture. This sort of "cultural Marxism" may not have affected the way many students acted before 1967 or 1968, but it certainly determined the way they thought about their situation. Revolution, class struggle, socialism, a mystique of the working class—the ideas were all there long before they took living form in May.

In the fall of 1967, the agitation over the war in Vietnam and over the growing university crisis converged. The Fouchet Plan was put into full operation just as the universities were swept by the largest wave yet of incoming students. Student political interest revived. There was not yet, however, anything one could pinpoint as "the movement." The only left-wing organizations on the scene were the *groupuscules.* These tiny groups, each with its own secatarian analysis of the "correct" tasks for the left, competed for student support. A few students joined one or another—especially the Trotskyist *Jeunesse Communiste Révolutionnaire* (JCR) *and Fédération des Étudiants Révolutionnaires* (FER) and the Maoist *Union de la Jeunesse Communiste (Marxiste-Léniniste).* Others passed through them, first looking for quick answers, then becoming more and more turned off by the sectarianism and sterility of these groups, and finally quitting. Most students, however left they considered themselves in principle, never bothered with the *groupuscules.*

The initial lead in the events which led to May was taken not by the *groupuscules* of the left, but by the national union of students (the *Union Nationale des Étudiants de France,* UNEF). In the first semester of the 1967–68 school year, the UNEF called for a week of protest activities around the crisis in the universities. Included was a brief student strike. At Nanterre, more than ten thousand students participated in the strike and won a few modest reforms. Most notably, joint student-faculty "committees of peers" were set up to discuss how to improve the university. But even this "victory" was short lived. The students soon discovered that the student-faculty committees had no power and were in little danger of even being listened to.

When it seemed that the UNEF wasn't going to accomplish much more, leadership passed over to less orthodox people. At Nanterre, especially, it was a small group of *les enragés* along with a number of *groupuscule* students who took the lead. All through the fall and winter, these people had been agitating the students and provoking the administration. They instigated a "sleep-in" in the women's dormitory to demand that men be permitted to visit women in their rooms. From the Germans they picked up the "go-in": they would enter a classroom and demand an immediate debate with the lecturer. Or they would occupy the lecture room next door to a regular class and deliver a counter-lecture or hold a critical discussion of the professor's lectures. The leftists also called for a boycott of the spring "partial" examinations. Exams, they argued, were the mainstay of the university's oppression and manipulation of the student. Exams give students their number, their price tag for the outside world. Exams force students to regurgitate the ideological nonsense their professors have pumped into them. With exams, they said, the university undertakes its primary act of violence against the autonomy of the students' existence. At Nanterre, many hundreds risked failing, in order to observe the boycott.

Meanwhile, the heat from Vietnam was beginning to be felt within the university as well as on the streets of Paris. Antiwar sentiment ran high, and in March 1968 offices of several American companies in Paris were hit by plastic explosives. The American Embassy became the target of stone-throwing demonstrators. As a result, six students were arrested, including two from Nanterre. On March 22, leftist students at Nanterre held a meeting to protest the arrests of their comrades. The *enragés* argued that an appropriate protest need not be directed against the police, who had performed the arrests. Arrests were the act of the whole system, of which the police were merely the armed wing. Therefore it was appropriate to respond by attacking the system in any of its institutions. Since they were in a university, one of the key institutions of the system, it was the university they should attack. And so 142 students, *groupuscule* and independent, occupied the administration building. They talked through the night, and decided to continue their movement, calling it after the day of the protest, the *Mouvement du 22 Mars* (the March 22nd Movement). As their next act, they planned a meeting to take place one week later—a giant discussion session.

The following week was a turbulent one at Nanterre. Students handed out leaflets and invaded classrooms to advertise the meeting. A far-right-wing group of students, *Occident* (whose mentors, revanchist paratroopers from the Algerian War, had taught them such political skills as hand-to-hand combat), threatened to disrupt the meeting. The rector of the university panicked. Late in the afternoon of the day preceding the meeting, he ordered the university closed for the next day and for the weekend immediately following, and attacked the "group of irresponsible students who for several months have disturbed classes and examinations." Minister of Education Peyrelitte predicted the decline of the movement: the *enragés,* he said, are "discrediting themselves more and more in the eyes of the mass of students...." The students were not scared off; they rescheduled the meeting for April 2.

Nothing builds a movement so rapidly as repression. On April 2, the 142 students who had formed the March 22nd Movement found that they had brought out twelve hundred students to the meeting. They took over a large amphitheater and began to talk. First they mapped out a program of educational and ideological work for the remainder of the academic year, featuring two "anti-imperialist" days. Then the students broke up into discussion groups, with orders to keep talking until a position had been worked out. There were sessions on anti-imperialist struggles, on culture and creativity, on critique of the university and the critical university, on eastern Europe, on student struggles and worker struggles, on examinations, and many other subjects.

But events were to prove that "educational and ideological work" was not enough. The struggle escalated rapidly. On April 3 a government committee announced that beginning in 1969, admissions to the university would no longer be unlimited. On April 19, following the attempted assassination of the German student leader Rudi Dutschke, two thousand students rallied in the Latin Quarter to demonstrate their solidarity with German SDS. Two days later, an extraordinary convention of the UNEF to elect a new president was disrupted and finally destroyed by rightists. On April 22, five thousand students demonstrated peacefully in solidarity with the Vietnamese people. On April 27, Dany Cohn-Bendit, one of the most prominent of the *enragés* at Nanterre, was arrested and questioned at length by the police. The next day, the right-wing *Occident* threatened to "crush the Bolshevik vermin."

As a result of these events, the first of the planned anti-imperialist days, May 2, found the students restless and tensed for possible violence between right and left. The rector at Nanterre decided once more to forestall trouble by closing the university, thus locking out the "anti-imperialists." The students, unable to meet in their own university, went to the Sorbonne in Paris to tell people what had happened.

On Friday, May 3, students gathered in the courtyard of the Sorbonne. Soon they found they were surrounded by policemen who claimed to be "protecting" them and refused to let anyone leave the courtyard. As it turned out, the cops were there under orders from Sorbonne Rector Roche to clear the whole faculty of students. Late that afternoon the police moved in and arrested almost six hundred students, with uncalled for brutality. The following Monday the students marched through the Latin Quarter, demanding the liberation of the arrested students. Twenty thousand strong, they chanted, "We are a *groupuscule,* a dozen *enragés.*" In the evening, the police moved in again, and in the battle that followed, four hundred more were arrested, and a total of six hundred policemen, students, and bystanders were injured.

Students' anger continued to mount. The next day a crowd estimated variously as thirty to sixty thousand marched. The UNEF and the union of university teachers called for a strike, demanding amnesty for those arrested, reopening of the faculties, and the withdrawal of the police from the Latin Quarter as a precondition to negotiations. But the government would not give, and by May 10, the students were determined to recapture the Latin Quarter. The government played its part, and ordered the riot police to clear the streets.

May 10, 1968, the "night of the barricades." Helmeted students overturned hundreds of cars and trucks. Gas tanks were emptied to fill Molotov cocktails and the vehicles pushed into the streets as barricades. When the police charged the students ignited the flimsy outer barricades and retreated behind a second, sturdier line. The police bombarded the students with tear gas grenades and concussion grenades and the students retaliated with cobblestones. "I never felt the gas," a veteran told us later, "I was never more alive." Occupants of the buildings lining the narrow streets threw down cold water and wet cloths for the gassed students. The police, perhaps rightly, considered everyone in the quarter their enemy. They beat anyone they could find in the streets, as well as any they could drag out of their apartments into the streets. The toll was 460 arrested, 367 injured, and unverified accounts of several dead in what had been the fiercest street fighting since the Liberation of Paris in 1944. When we were in Paris four weeks later, the Latin Quarter looked like a newly occupied colony: boarded-up store fronts, gutted cafes, and pitted streets, all well patrolled by squads of police armed with submachine guns.

Government violence had gone too far this time. Thousands of ordinary citizens had watched students being beaten systematically with clubs and rifle butts, dragged through the streets by their hair, kicked to unconsciousness, or drenched with liquid tear gas. The government hastily tried to retreat before the enraged populace. Faculties would be reopened, and the police withdrawn from the Latin Quarter. Premier Pompidou promised that the cases of the arrested students would be reconsidered. But it was too late to make amends. As the police withdrew, students rushed back in and re-took the streets. As the faculties opened, students moved in and occupied them. As arrested students and workers were released, they rejoined their comrades in the Latin Quarter. Then came the nearly irreversible step towards revolution: the biggest national confederations of trade unions, the Communist-controlled CGT (*Confédération Générale du Travail*) and the independent CFDT (*Confédération Française Démocratique du Travail*) called for a one-day general strike. Monday, May 13, was set aside to protest police brutality and to raise the workers' own demands for higher wages, shorter hours, and union rights.

Monday came, and something like a million people demonstrated, marching through the streets of Paris. What had begun on May 2 as a student anti-imperialist day had become on May 13 a vast anti-government demonstration. At the end of the massive procession, despite the opposition of the trade union leadership, the March 22nd Movement called for a collective discussion of the day's events and of the tasks ahead. Many workers obeyed the union leaders and went home, but thousands of others marched to the Eiffel Tower to join the students. On the Champ de Mars at the base of the tower, the two crowds mingled and talked well into the night.

Tuesday evening brought electrifying news. The Sud-Aviation

plant, near Nantes, was not going back to work. The workers had seized their factory. From Nantes the occupation movement spread like wildfire. The next day, while the students were occupying the Odéon Theater for use as a vast public debating hall, workers at the Renault factories, first at Cléon and then at Flins, occupied their factories. Factory after factory, studios, labs, train stations, work places of every kind were occupied by their workers. Even fourteen-year-old children occupied their schools. By the beginning of the following week, the country was paralyzed. Ten million workers, two-thirds of the entire work force, were on strike. The demands in some quarters escalated from higher wages to "workers', peasants', and students' power," and *autogestion* (workers' self-management).

France teetered on the edge of full-scale revolution. Everywhere people met—in cafes, ex-theaters, ex-schools, factories, streets—the topics of discussion were the same: grievances against de Gaulle; *autogestion;* self-defense of occupied factories; have we gone too far? have we gone far enough? Every day brought new rumors: that de Gaulle was massing troops in Alsace, that the police were ready to join the strike, that the government buildings in Paris would be captured by the workers. At Cannes some of France's leading film directors disrupted the film festival. In Paris, students and workers clashed almost daily with the police. In the countryside, peasants carted their produce to the workers in occupied factories. Through-out it all, the harried bureaucrats of the CGT haggled night and day for wage increases and better working conditions. After many days they brought a "settlement" back to the workers only to be hooted down, and sent back, sheepishly, for more. Neither party to the negotiations, the trade unions nor the government, seemed to know what to do. One rumor had it that senior government officials were bundling up their papers and preparing to flee. On the international markets, the mighty franc trembled in the winds of revolution.

In the last week of May, de Gaulle finally made his stand. If the government was going to change, he was going to be the one to change it. He dissolved the National Assembly and called for new elections. The mood of the people shifted rapidly. Many solid citizens, shopkeepers, white collar workers, etc. began to feel that the holiday was over. Revolution is fun for a while, but if you can't count on the electricity and the corner bar is running out of cigarettes, well, maybe things have gone too far. Besides, de Gaulle might have a point about the danger of "totalitarian communism."

Actually, as de Gaulle must have realized, the Communist party was the least of his worries. All along, the CGT and the Communist party had done their best to cool things, knowing full well that they would fall in the face of the workers' demand for power before the government did. So when de Gaulle called for elections, the party cheerfully repressed all memory of Lenin and decided to continue the struggle in electoral politics, not in the factories and streets. They pressured the workers, sometimes ruthlessly, to go back to work and forget about *autogestion.* They condemned students and militant workers as "adventurists" or "provocateurs." In case that wasn't enough to keep students away, CGT goons were posted at the factory gates of some factories near Paris. Thousands of workers, appeased by wage increases or demoralized by the collapse of their leadership, began to filter back to work. Thousands of very unrevolutionary people, caught up in the forward thrust of May, came to their normal senses and realized they didn't want a revolution. Thousands of waverers, frightened by the violence and chaos of May, decided to vote for de Gaulle, their only bastion against anarchy. The threat of revolution faded into anecdotes, and, in late June, the Gaullists won a landslide victory.

The last holdouts were the students. They weren't driven out of their occupied buildings by any misgivings about the revolution, but by the police. When the tide went out in June, a revolutionary contingent was left. There were thousands of students who could never again sit through a lecture, thousands of students who could never fit themselves into the narrow limits of a profession. Whatever they had been in April was forgotten in June. Again and again in conversations we heard the sentence, "Before May I was a chemist," or "an existentialist," or "a kid." What happened before May, the events and issues leading up to the barricades, could have been a whole chapter in the story of another country's student movement. To the French students, all that was preface. It was important because it led to May, but everything that follows, follows from May.

To understand the organizations and the people who emerged from May as revolutionary, you have to try to understand how haphazard the whole thing was. There was no cell of revolutionaries, no party organization, propelling events to a final confrontation. The workers vacillated between loyalty to the Communist party and the gambler's impulse to keep pushing for a win. The party scrambled to keep a millimeter ahead of the workers, without seeming too forward to the government.

The students were not, in any traditional sense, organized at all. Their "organization" was the March 22nd Movement, which spread from Nanterre faster and farther than its adherents could have traveled. In fact, March 22nd wasn't an organization at all; it was a name, a rallying cry, a style, a way of acting. If you were active and you liked what you had heard of March 22nd, then you were "in" March 22nd. It was at any time the sum of the people who were acting and the embodiment of their ideas. If March 22nd has to be classified as an organization, then we would call it multi-tendency in ideology and anarchistic in form. It could hardly have been otherwise, since it did not grow by recruitment, but by accretion of new groups and new individuals as they moved into action. The test of March 22nd's "organizational" strength came in June, when the government ordered it, along with several other groups, to dissolve. Since there were no officers, no members, and no membership cards, the dissolution order had no effect on March 22nd activities. (As we shall see, it was the decline of the action period of May and June that eventually led to March 22nd's decline.)

The local mode of action during May and June also emerged in the course of the struggle. After May 13, *Comités d'Action* (Action Committees) sprang up in universities and schools, in factories and in neighborhoods. Groups of foreigners such as Algerian, Portuguese, Spanish, and Italian workers, and even Americans, started *Comités d'Action.* By early June, there were three or four hundred active action committees, mainly in the Paris area. Each committee undertook the tasks that seemed appropriate to its constituency and its abilities. Thus, an occupied faculty at the university would have committees for propaganda, posters, internal education, cooperation with workers, and sometimes even an overall committee coordinating the others. A neighborhood in Paris would have action committees raising money, putting up posters, distributing leaflets, organizing people for demonstrations, or selling movement newspapers. The action committees were coordinated only loosely and sporadically.

They would meet and discuss possible common actions, the overall orientation of the action committees, the tasks to be done. Specific directives were not handed down to individual committees. Instead, each group took on the responsibility of doing what it felt it could handle.

The principle that kept all these diverse groups together was "unity on action, diversity on ideology." There was no attempt to hammer out a common program or detailed set of demands. For example, most of the action committees opposed de Gaulle's special June elections and condemned the Communist party's participation as "reformist." But the grounds for opposition varied from committee to committee and from neighborhood to neighborhood. Some argued that elections were a diversion, a way of dividing the workers and diverting attention away from the real problems. Others argued that elections were not democratic because young people, eighteen to twenty-one, who had played such a prominent role thus far, could not vote. Others pointed out that the election laws were rigged so that the left parties ended up with fewer representatives in parliament than their strength among the electorate warranted. Others argued that elections were irrelevant in any case, that representational forms, however egalitarian, are really antidemocratic, that only direct participation without intermediaries was really democratic. In short, the opposition to participation in the elections ranged from broad ideological rejection of electoral action as a revolutionary tactic to narrow tactical opposition to *this* election. But this diversity did not prevent the action committees from working together for a boycott of the elections. The action committees shared an antigovernment, anticapitalist ideology; they could cooperate in working against the government and against capitalism. That was all, but in May, it seemed to be enough.

*   *   *

March 22nd never really had a strategy or saw the need for one. They did have a tactic: direct action. Multiplied many times over it becomes, we guess, a strategy itself. March 22nd students did not see themselves as "leaders," as an "avant garde" who go out and carefully organize to "raise the consciousness" of the workers. Instead, they saw themselves as having been the "active minority" which "plays the part of a permanent fermenting agent, encouraging action without claiming to lead. . . . It is spontaneity which permits the thrust forward, and not the slogans or directives of a leading group" (Cohn-Bendit). In May, this ferment began in the university, among students, but this need not always be true. Next time inspiration could strike some other group.

The mechanisms of "fermenting" are confrontation and "exemplary action." You act on a set of issues, a situation. By acting you provoke a confrontation which exposes the real nature of the situation and forces people to take sides. For instance, confronting university officials on a university issue may lead to their responding by calling the police. This exposes the way in which the university is dependent on the power of the state, and reveals the latent violence and authoritarianism in the day-to-day social relations which most people normally accept.

Another, perhaps more trivial, example comes from the early May days at Nanterre: meetings of students and of professors were held simultaneously but separately in adjoining auditoriums. The professors hesitantly proposed that the students send in a representative to explain to them what they were thinking and doing. To the students, this request smacked of professorial aloofness and authoritarianism. The chairman of the student session yanked open the door between the two auditoriums and angrily told the professors that if they wanted to talk and to cooperate in any way with the students, they must immediately come in and meet with them as equals, *en masse.* If they weren't willing to do that, they should forget the whole thing—go back to their academic studies and forget that anything was happening. "Take it or leave it." The professors, somewhat shamefacedly, took it—they came in and joined with the students. Once people have been forced to choose, to take sides, then according to March 22nd, you can begin to talk to them more reasonably.

To March 22nd, direct action was not just a lively new style of protest. The pattern of direct action was not seen as a reaction to events, but as the *creation* of events. Thus, the importance of acting went beyond the narrow aims of any particular action. For action shows people that they can take their fate into their own hands. Action shakes people loose from old habits of inertia and transforms them from objects of history to agents of history. There is no such thing, the activists insisted, as "being" anticapitalist or "being" revolutionary. Revolutionary militance is not a state of grace or a salaried position in the Communist party; it is a way of acting. What is more, it is a way of acting *now*. You don't have to sit around and wait for the appropriate "objective conditions" anymore than you have to wait for a call from the Central Committee. "Objective conditions" for revolution are something to create, not something to wait for. In these terms, the students didn't see themselves as leading the workers at any time, only as setting an example. As Cohn-Bendit said, "The active minority was able . . . to light the first fuse. . . . But that's all. The others could follow or not follow. It happens that they followed."

The value of "exemplary action" seemed to be confirmed in May. Students acted, setting the example, and the workers proceeded to act on their own. But as the movement began to collapse in June, some students had time to reflect back on pre-May history. They pointed out that the isolated cases of direct action in the months and years before May 1968 hadn't caught on outside the university at all, much less snowballed into near-revolution. And in June all the attempts to restimulate the lagging workers' struggle were failing. The workers were slowly, inexorably, dropping out of the battle. Maybe there *was* something special about May 1968, even "objectively" special. They began to accept the idea that mass struggle can only be created on some sort of substratum of objective conditions. In between the moments of apocalyptic mass action, there would have to be intervals of minor confrontations and sustained organizing.

*   *   *

Words lie heavy on the March 22nd Movement. No amount of analysis could tell as much about March 22nd revolutionary views as a day in Paris in May or June. Whatever it meant on the world money market, or to NATO, or to Premier Pompidou, May was above all a creative breakthrough, a triumph of imagination. For the first time, thousands of students, after years of the steady discipline of school, dared to dream and to act. Many were serious revolutionaries, but no one was grim. "Distrust sad people," said one graffito! *"La révolution, c'est la joie."* To talk to one of the March 22nd activists was

FIGURE 3. The youth revolution in the West: charging police in riot gear club a
young French demonstrator during the "May Days" of 1968. (*Gamma*)

FIGURE 4. Marching still: young protesters surge through the streets of Paris, 1968. *(Gamma)*

to talk to someone who was high. Only after you had spent some time in an occupied building and developed a contact high of your own could you begin to understand.

The École des Beaux Arts, renamed by its occupiers the "Ex-École des Beaux Arts," looked like the scene of some unearthly festival. The black, fortress-like walls were slashed with red flags and covered with posters, slogans, and long passages from the works of various revolutionary heroes. The statues surrounding the courtyard had been painted, decorated, or given red flags to hold. But liberated art isn't all hedonism. Upstairs in the Ex-École, dozens of ex(?)-students worked frantically to get out the day's supply of revolutionary posters, which would appear on the walls in every quarter of Paris the next day. Others were heading off to the factories to talk to the striking workers, or were writing tracts to be handed out all over the city.

At the annex to the faculty of letters at Censier, the walls were covered with poems. In the amphitheaters of the Sorbonne, debate went on into the night. Sundays, thousands of workers crowded into the Sorbonne courtyard to talk with the students. An eyewitness account, published in an English pamphlet on the events, described it like this:

> Those who had never dared say anything suddenly felt their thoughts to be the most important thing in the world—and said so. The shy became communicative. The helpless and isolated suddenly discovered that collective power lay in their hands. . . . A tremendous surge of community and cohesion gripped those who had previously seen themselves as isolated and impotent puppets, dominated by institutions they could neither control nor understand. . . . An inscription on a wall sums it up perfectly: "Déjà dix jours de bonheur" *(Already ten days of happiness).*

A year before May, a widely read pamphlet put out by the International Situationists in Strasbourg, said it like this: True proletarian revolution is *"une fête."* "Play is the ultimate rationale of this fête, to live outside of dead time and to act without inhibitions."

The demands of May were only the verbalization of the revolutionary mood. One word sums them all up: *autogestion. Autogestion* translates somewhat pallidly as "self-management," but it can only be defined by examples. In factories, *autogestion* meant control by workers. In schools, it meant control by students and teachers (assuming, of course, that the old hierarchical student-teacher relationship would be destroyed, and that teachers and students would study together). In the family, it meant an end to patriarchal domination of wives and children. In fact, in any institution involving more than one person, *autogestion* meant direct democratic cotrol by everyone involved. The mechanisms of control need not be carefully prescribed, since they would be flexible and changing with the needs and interests of the participants. However, they should never be merely representational—the quickest way to give up power is to hand it over to a representative. Direct democracy, direct participation in all decisionmaking is the key.

This demand for *autogestion,* the style of struggle, the attitudes toward organization and toward organizing together define the utopia of the students. Revolution to them was not to be just a transfer of power, but an *end* to power, a freeing of people to grow and to do what it is possible for them to do, as more and more *becomes* possible. There was no talk of "when we run society. . . ."—society is not something to be "run" but something to be participated in. The utopia "after the revolution" is the continuation of the revolution, the continual opening up of new ways to be human. To quote Cohn-Bendit once more: "It isn't a matter of . . . figuring out how to make 'the revolution'. . . . We are moving toward a perpetual change in society, spurred on, at each stage, by revolutionary actions." . . .

Back in June, a March 22nd activist told us that the students might not be able to carry through the revolution, might even become counterrevolutionary. "But it doesn't matter," he continued, "because the sixteen-year-olds, the thirteen-year-olds, are revolutionary now. They will push us out of the way and go on by themselves someday."

III GENERATIONAL REVOLT : A FORCE IN HISTORY?

Lewis S. Feuer

GENERATIONAL UPHEAVAL AS A PATHOLOGICAL FACTOR IN HISTORY

Professor Lewis Feuer (b. 1912), currently of the University of Toronto, has taught and written on philosophical, psychological, and sociological subjects, as well as on historical themes. His books include Psychoanalysis and Ethics *(1955),* The Scientific Intellectual *(1963), and the volume from which the following article is taken,* The Conflict of Generations: The Character and Significance of Student Movements *(1969). The influence of several of Feuer's other scholarly interests, most notably psychology and sociology, is evident in what follows. So is his essentially negative verdict on the Youth Revolution as a force in history.*

This is a book about the workings of the ethical, idealistic spirit in human history. For of all social movements, those composed of students have been characterized by the highest degree of selflessness, generosity, compassion, and readiness for self-sacrifice. And this is also a book about how the idealistic spirit has done violence to itself and to others, and has been transmuted into a destructive force in human history. Our narratives will tell of the eternal duality which pervades historical movements.

The distinctive character of student movements arises from the union in them of motives of youthful love, on the one hand, and those springing from the conflict of generations on the other. We shall thus be inquiring into the complex psychological origins of human idealism, for we cannot understand the destructive pole of student movements until we have brought to light the obscure unconscious workings of generational conflict. Then perhaps we shall know why student movements have been fated to tragedy.

To their own consciousness, students in student movements have been the bearers of a higher ethic than the surrounding society. Certainly in their essential character student movements are historical forces which are at odds with the "social system." A society is never altogether a social system precisely because such contrasystemic "unsocialized" agencies such as student movements arise. As Walter Weyl said: "Adolescence is the true day for revolt, the day when obscure forces, as mysterious as growth, push us, trembling, out of our narrow lives into the wide throbbing life beyond self." No society ever altogether succeeds in molding the various psychological types which comprise it to conform to its material, economic requirements. If there were a genuine correspondence between the material, economic base and the psychological superstructure, then societies would be static social systems, and basic social change would not take place. In every society, however, those psychological types and motivations which the society suppresses become the searching agents of social change. Thus psycho-ethical motives, which are not only independent of the socioeconomic base but actually contrary to the economic ethics that the social system requires, become primary historical forces.

The Russian revolutionary student movement is the classic case of the historic workings of the ethical consciousness. When in the 1860s and 1870s several thousand student youth, inspired by feelings of guilt and responsibility for the backward people, embarked on their "back-to-the-people" movement, it was an unparalleled collective act of selfless idealism. The anarchist Prince Kropotkin conveyed its spirit in notable words:

> Thousands and thousands of Russian youth—the best part of it—were doing the same. Their watchword was "V narod" (To the people; be the people). During the years 1860–1865, in nearly every wealthy family a bitter struggle was going on between the fathers, who wanted to maintain the old traditions, and the sons and daughters.... Young men left the military service, the counter, the shop, and flocked to the university towns. Girls bred in the most aristocratic families rushed penniless to St. Petersburg, Moscow, and Kieff, eager to learn a profession.... Now they wanted to utilize it, not for their own personal enjoyment, but for carrying to the people the knowledge that had emancipated them.... Gradually, they came to the idea that the only way was to settle amongst the people, and to live the people's life.

The students' ethical consciousness was utterly independent of class interests and class position. The largest single group among those who were arrested in the back-to-the-people movement from

1873 to 1877 were children of the nobility. They could have availed themselves of the ample openings in the governmental bureaucracy. Instead, many of them chose a path of self-sacrifice and suffering. Rebuffed by the peasants, the revolutionary student youth later gave themselves to the most extreme self-immolation of individual terrorism. And when terrorism failed to produce the desired social change, circles of student intellectuals provided the first nuclei of the Social Democratic party. Lenin aptly said that the intellectuals brought a socialist consciousness to the workers, who by themselves would not have gone beyond trade union aspirations. The intellectuals Lenin referred to were indeed largely the self-sacrificing revolutionary students.

The ethic of the Russian student generations was not shaped by the institutional requirements of the society. The universal theme of generational revolt, which cuts across all societies, produced in Russia a "conflict of generations" of unparalleled intensity because of special social circumstances. The Russian students lived their external lives in a social reality which was absolutist, politically tyrannical, and culturally backward; internally, on the other hand, they lived in a milieu imbued with Western cultural values. Their philosophical and idealistic aims transcended the social system, and were out of keeping with it; the philosophical culture and the social system were at odds with each other, in "contradiction." The revolutionists, we might say, were historical transcendentalists, not historical materialists. The government opened universities to provide recruits for its bureaucracy. Some students followed the appointed path, but the universities became the centers not only for bureaucratic education but for revolutionary dedication. The idealistic student as a psychological type was recalcitrant to the specifications of the social system.

The civil rights movement in the United States has likewise owed much to students as the bearers of an ethical vocation in history. A wave of sit-ins which spread through Negro college towns began on February 1, 1960, when four freshmen from the all-Negro Agricultural and Technical College at Greensboro, North Carolina, sat down at the lunch counter of the local Woolworth dime store. The surrounding community was puzzled that it was precisely "the best educated, the most disciplined and cultured—and essentially middle-class—Negro students" who took the self-sacrificing initiative. Moreover, it was recognized generally, to use one writer's words, that "for the time being it is the students who have given a lift to the established civil rights organizations rather than the other way around." Then in the next years came movements which resembled even more the "back-to-the-people" movement of the Russian studentry. The Freedom Riders of 1961, the several hundred white students in the Mississippi Summer Project of 1964 risking their lives to establish Freedom Schools among the Negroes, were descendants in spirit of the Russian students of the preceding century.

Nonetheless, the duality of motivation which has spurred student movements has always borne its duality of consequence. On the one hand, student movements during the past 150 years have been the bearers of a higher ethic for social reconstruction, of altruism, and of generous emotion. On the other hand, with all the uniformity of a sociological law, they have imposed on the political process a choice of means destructive both of self and of the goals which presumably were sought. Suicidalism and terrorism have both been invariably present in student movements. A youth-weighted rate of suicide is indeed characteristic of all countries in which large-scale revolutionary student movements are found. In what we might call a "normal" country, or one in which there is a "generational equilibrium," "suicide," as Louis Dublin said, "is much more prevalent in advanced years than during youth." But a "normal" country is one without a revolutionary student movement. Where such movements have existed, where countries are thus characterized by a severe conflict of generations, the rate of suicide has been highest precisely for the youthful group. Nihilism has tended to become the philosophy of student movements not only because it constitutes a negative critique of society; it is also a self-critique that is moved by an impulse toward self-annihilation.

Every historical era tends to have its own most significant choices. In the 1940s, for example, the yogi and commissar, as Arthur Koestler phrased it, posed a critical ethical dilemma for many people. But the double-edged choice which confronts student movements is perhaps best expressed in the title of an essay by Ivan Turgenev, "Hamlet and Don Quixote," written as the Russian student movement was being born. For Hamlet, with his negation, destructive doubt, and intellect turned against himself, was indeed the suicidal pole in the Russian student character, whereas Don Quixote, with his undoubting devotion to an ideal, his readiness to fight for the oppressed and to pit himself against all social institutions, represented the messianic, back-to-the-people component. The Russian student activist, like his later successors, oscillated between these polar impulses; rejected by the people, he would often find in terrorism a sort of synthesis, for thereby he could assail a social institution in a personalized form and hurl against it all the aggressive passions which menaced himself. Don Quixote thus became a student terrorist. When his ventures in terror miscarried, his passions turned against himself; in the last act, he was Hamlet destroying himself. Yet Turgenev believed that if there were no more Don Quixotes the book of history would be closed.

The student movement in Russia inscribed terrorism on its banner. Often it combined terrorism and suicide, for it became the mark of a selfless political murder to destroy oneself at the same time. The long roll of assassinations and attempted assassinations of czars, ministers of education, police chiefs, generals, grand dukes, ministers of interior, was simultaneously a roll call of student and ex-student suicides and martyrdoms. Dmitri Karakozov, Andrei Zhelyabov, Sophia Pervoskaya, Alexander Ulyanov, S. V. Balmashov, Ivan Kaliaev, P. Karpovich, and Yegor Sazonov wrote their self-sacrificial names in history beside those of Alexander II, Alexander III, Minister of Interior Sipiagin, the Grand Duke Serge Alexandrovich, commander of the Moscow military region, Minister of Public Instruction Bogolepov, and Minister of Interior von Plehve. What was true of the Russian student movement was likewise true of the German student movement of 1815 to 1819, and the Bosnian student movement as well in the years before the First World War. This predilection for an ethic in which the end justified any means whatsoever, including terrorism, the ethic of an elitist amorality, cut across all cultures, as we shall see, and was common to all student movements.

In later chapters we shall undertake to show how the component of generational conflict in student movements has made for an amorality in the choice of political means. We may mention briefly, however, some salient facts in the history of student movements and the hypotheses they suggest concerning the bearing of student movements on the evolution of modern society. In so doing, we shall anticipate somewhat our later narrative. Karl Follen, the first student

leader in modern history, taught his entranced followers in the
Burschenschaft in 1819 that all means were sanctified by the glorious
end of the "Christian German Republic." His influence proved
greater than that of the professors in the German universities who
tried to inculcate the ethic of the Kantian categorical imperative. One
of Follen's selfless followers took his words in the most consequen-
tial sense and on March 23, 1819, stabbed to death the dramatist and
political reactionary Kotzebue. All Germany was shaken by the deed.
The assassin, Karl Sand, tried unsuccessfully to kill himself at the
same time. Prior to the killing he had sketched a portrait of himself
kneeling on the church steps and pressing a dagger into his heart.
The student activists hailed Sand's deed as "a sign of that which will
and must come." They came in droves to see his execution, and they
purchased as sacred relics the boards on which Sand's blood was
splattered. For years afterward, the members of the Heidelberg
Burschenschaft would gather in a cottage built from the scaffold's
timbers as guests of Sand's executioner. It was a rite for a dualistic
death wish, terrorism and suicidalism, altruism and aggression.

In Bosnia the students made a cult of Zherajitch, who in 1910 had
tried to murder the governor and then killed himself. "Young Bosnia
had no fixed program or stable organization," wrote a later participant, "but they had a specific ethic of their own, a very altruistic
one . . . more like living saints. . . ." Zherajitch had written, "We are
a new generation, we are new men in every way." The student movement took this to heart in a series of assassinations of the old men.
Almost all of the attempted assassinations of Austrian officials between 1910 and 1914 were by members of the student movement. A
pamphlet, "The Death of a Hero," by Vladimir Gatchinovitch, became
their bible. Then followed killings and a series of attempts which
culminated in the assassination of the Archduke Franz Ferdinand in
June 1914 by the student Gavrilo Princip, working as a member of
a three-student team, all under twenty years of age. Princip too tried
to commit suicide with potassium cyanide but failed. As we shall
later see, several months of psychiatric interviews with Princip as
well as the testimony of his close friend show him to have been
laboring under the severe strain of generational conflict—intense
love for his mother which he is described as "confessing," combined with hostility toward his father. His fantasy life was filled with
images of assassination. Gavrilo Princip acted out the heroic politics

of his struggle with his parents on the stage of history and imposed his pattern of self-destruction on most of Europe and the rest of the world.

This brings us to what is most significant for the theory of social change—namely, the consequences of the superimposition of a student movement on a nationalistic, peasant, or labor movement. Every student movement tries to attach itself to a "carrier" movement of more major proportions—such as a peasant, labor, nationalist, racial, or anti-colonial movement. We may call the latter the "carrier" movements by way of analogy with the harmonic waves superimposed on the carrier wave in physics. But the superimposition of waves of social movements differs in one basic respect from that of physical movements. The student movement gives a new qualitative character and direction to social change. It imparts to the carrier movement a quality of emotion, dualities of feeling, which would otherwise have been lacking. Emotions issuing from the students' unconscious, and deriving from the conflict of generations, impose or attach themselves to the underlying political carrier movement, and deflect it in irrational directions. Given a set of alternative paths—rational or irrational—for realizing a social goal—the influence of a student movement will be toward the use of the most irrational means to achieve the end. Student movements are thus what one would least expect—among the most irrationalist in history.

Generational revolt is not a necessary ingredient for basic social change. Indeed, revolutionary change has taken place in modern times without a concomitant involvement of a younger generation in conflict with an older generation. On the whole, for instance, as we shall see, a generational equilibrium has prevailed in American history. The advent of the Civil War was not preceded by a student abolitionist movement of any proportions in the colleges. Dartmouth, Middlebury, Harvard, were without such societies, and Harvard as a whole supported Daniel Webster in the Compromise of 1850. Harvard through its history underwent cycles of generational insurrection, but that element of the moral de-authoritization of the older generation so essential to the rise of a student movement never emerged. Student grievances did not merge with an ideological discontent and social cause to constitute a student movement. Where such a superimposition of a student movement on the processes of social change has taken place, the evidence is overwhelming that the chances for a rational evolution and achievement of social goals have been adversely affected. In Germany, the effect of Karl Follen's movement was, as Kuno Francke said, to set back for a generation the liberal aspirations of the German people.

In the case of the Russian student movement, it was the opinion of the most distinguished anarchist, Peter Kropotkin, that "the promulgation of a constitution was extremely near at hand during the last few months of the life of Alexander II." Kropotkin greatly admired the idealism of the Russian students, yet he felt their intervention had been part of an almost accidental chain of circumstances that had defeated Russia's hopes. Bernard Pares, the historian, who also witnessed the masochist-terrorist characteristics of the Russian students at first hand, wrote, "The bomb that killed Alexander II put an end to the faint beginnings of Russian constitutionalism." A half-hour before the czar set out on his last journey on March 1, 1881, he approved the text of a decree announcing the establishment of a commission likely to lead to the writing of a constitution. "I have consented to this measure," said Alexander II, "although I do not conceal from myself the fact that this is the first step toward a constitution." Instead, the students' acts of czar-killing and self-killing brought into Russian politics all the psychological overtones of sons destroying their fathers; their dramatic idealism projected on a national political scale the emotional pattern of "totem and taboo," the revolt and guilt of the primal sons Freud described. People turned in shock from the sick, self-destructive students; the liberals felt as if they had had the ground pulled out from under them. The Social Revolutionary party, which was most representative of the peasants, and which had the largest vote in November 1917, gave its endorsement for many years to student terrorism. Thereby the party which might have been the chief vehicle for rational evolution gave its blessing to pathological politics. As Professor Jesse D. Clarkson writes, "In retrospect, one may be convinced that the long series of assassinations of governors, ministers, and police chiefs . . . impeded, rather than aided, the attainment of the party's objectives."

No social scientist, of course, would suggest that Gavrilo Princip's deed was a sufficient condition for the outbreak of the First World War. All the familiar rivalries and hatreds among nations were involved too. Yet for two generations a tradition of peace had been taking root in Europe. Peaceful social democratic movements were gaining in influence; great figures, men of peace such as Jean Jaurès, were gaining renown and influence in Europe. It was likely indeed that Russia, if it were spared the stress of war, would continue rapidly to evolve in a liberal capitalist direction. There was hope in Europe that a rational society would emerge, a society whose prophets were Wells, Shaw, Anatole France, Norman Angell. The equilibrium of Europe was shaky, but the roots of a growing stability were there too. In Russia, the studentry was beginning to put aside the politics of generational revolt. Yet its echo in the Balkans was strong enough to upset the European balance of power and mind, and to set moving a self-destructive chain of events. Gavrilo Princip, who dreamed of killing policemen, finally achieved his place as a father-destroyer, a hero in history, even though it also meant the destruction of himself and the maiming of European civilization.

Herbert Moller

REBELLIOUS YOUTH AS A FORCE FOR CHANGE

Herbert Moller (b. 1909), professor of history at Boston University, has been particularly interested in social and economic history and in demography. His best known work is Effects of Population Changes on Society, 1500 to 1800 *(1942). The depth of Moller's demographic understanding lends considerable weight to his analysis of youth as a significant slice of the population in modern times. In Moller's view, the Youth Revolution, however deplorable in some of its aspects, does represent a potentially powerful force in history.*

The unprecedented number of young people in the world today can be isolated as one of the crucial reality factors conditioning political

From Herbert Moller, "Youth as a Force in the Modern World," *Comparative Studies in Society and History* 10 (1968): 237, 254–260. Reprinted by permission of the Cambridge University Press. Footnotes omitted.

and cultural developments. Age distribution is only one demographic variable in the complex of social and political life, but the tremendous growth of world population in the twentieth century has magnified its dynamic potentialities. To gain perspective, it will be useful to briefly consider the role of youth in the light of historical experience. . . .

In any community the presence of a large number of adolescents and young adults influences the temper of life; and the greater the proportion of young people the greater the likelihood of cultural and political change. "If poor aging peasants can be left to misery or even starvation without serious political consequences, the case is different with the young generation." Age composition, to be sure, constitutes only one determinant in the functioning of society; therefore it cannot be assumed that a large proportion of young people makes the same implications for every nation, nor even for every poor and starving nation. Too often, however, a direct and exclusive correlation between the incidence of violence and of poverty is taken for granted. This impression is easily created by the observation that outbursts of violence are more frequent, nationally, in disadvantaged neighborhoods and, internationally, in underdeveloped and overpopulated countries. But since poor and crowded neighborhoods as well as underdeveloped countries have high proportions of young people, age composition must be considered as a major coefficient in the incidence of violent behavior.

For instance, the struggle of the American Negroes in the 1960s has been borne almost exclusively by Negro youth. Since the Second World War, American Negroes have not become poorer in absolute terms, especially not in the big northern cities where the greater part of the struggle against white society has taken place. But Negroes have become younger. The larger contingent of Negro teenagers cannot be accounted the only factor in the explosive discontent that led to riots, for the widening gap between white and Negro incomes and white and Negro unemployment played an important part. But the presence of youth in large numbers stood out as a factor of crucial importance: the attitudes of the young contrasted sharply with those of the older Negroes, who were, for the most part, too dispirited to bring themselves to go out and demonstrate, to vote in city elections, or even to meet suppression and violence with violence.

Class antagonism is another factor whose importance in revolutionary change is deflated, once attention is directed to the role of youth. The widely held assumption that political revolutions are caused by class struggles or are synonymous with class struggles has been challenged in the past few years by historical research on the Puritan Revolution, the French Revolution, the rise of National Socialism in Germany, and other more recent governmental upheavals. Smail's unique study of the early Indonesian Revolution, as it worked on the local level, led him to conclude that class factors were irrelevant and that "the main distinction between the radicals and the moderates of the Indonesian Revolution was one of generations. . . . The *pemuda* [youth] movement as a whole was the most characteristic expression of the times; it drew in young men of every kind of background—rural and urban, *santri* [devout Muslims] and secular, educated and illiterate."

At the national level, in Djakarta, the revolution was a struggle between the foreign Dutch and a domestic elite; but the sentiment of nationalism was not essential for the revolutionary activities and the replacement of officials. "In this period the revolutionary process worked with the same vigor in the rural areas, where the Dutch and the British did not appear at all and where nationalism as such was of little significance." In the Indonesian Revolution the most decisive factors were the population pressure that had been growing ever stronger during the course of the twentieth century, the weakening of the traditional power structure through the events of the Pacific war, and the activism of youth stimulated during the Japanese occupation. Similarly, the 1964 revolution in Zanzibar had for its official aim the replacement of an Arab by a Negro elite; but the rise of young adults—even though of Arab origin—to positions of power was an equally important, if less well-publicized aspect.

Historical evidence appears to indicate that the subversion of any established government, if not accomplished by coup d'état, requires a movement that cuts across social classes; and whether such a movement is directed against a native or a foreign elite, young people provide the driving force and often, to a large extent, the intellectual and organizational leadership. "Most of the nationalistic movements in the Middle East, Asia, and Africa have consisted of young people, students, or officers who rebelled against their elders. . . . At the same time there usually has developed a specific youth consciousness and ideology that intensifies the nationalistic movement to 'rejuvenate' the country." As a result many of the newly formed nations have what Robert C. Tucker has called "movement regimes," i.e., governments under single-party auspices and based on a revolutionary mass movement.

Since the world population is bound to grow very rapidly in the coming decades, the absolute number of young people will increase tremendously. In many countries their proportion to the older age groups will rise, until finally declining birth rates and mass longevity will reverse the present trend. The social and economic consequences of large youth cohorts, of course, vary greatly among different societies. Broadly speaking, it can be said that developed and prosperous countries can cope best with the need for larger educational facilities, the effects on the labor market, and changes in consumption. These same countries can also profit more readily from the advantages of a young population, from their physical vigor, intellectual flexibility, and educability. A dynamic and developed society can best stimulate, utilize, and reward the creative originality that belongs to those under thirty-five. A youthful population represents a great reservoir of inventiveness and potential accomplishment. However, most societies throughout history have been too poor in capital resources, too rigid and monopolistic in their social structure, and too limited in their educational facilities to avail themselves of these human potentials, a fact which still holds true of most societies today. The overwhelming majority of human talent remains unrecognized and goes to waste. Unfortunately underdeveloped societies produce underdeveloped personalities, both intellectually and emotionally.

Irrespective of social and economic conditions, an increase in the number of youth in any society involves an increase in social turbulence. Young people are conspicuously inclined to take risks, to expose themselves and others to danger, and tend to engage in socially disruptive behavior. Discounting the considerable variation from nation to nation, long-range statistics confirm the fact that everywhere in the Western world males between fifteen and twenty-nine years of age commit more crimes against property and more homicides than the older population. As a rule they commit fewer suicides, with the notable exception of soldiers and, in recent decades, college students, who have higher suicide rates than the remainder of their coevals. But the aggressiveness of male adolescents and young adults is for the most part directed outwards, a finding which represents one of the most pronounced differences between younger and older men that are statistically measurable. . . .

Any judgment on the utility or disutility of the influence of the young and of youthful mass movements on society must consider an array of problems: Who are the elites with a mass appeal to youth? What percentage of the young population is alienated? What are the reasons for their alienation? To what extent are force and terrorism needed to effectuate or prevent certain changes? What are the social and human costs of change, and what are the costs of the preservation of the status quo? And so on.

Some general observations can be made regarding the methods of political action that have been employed by more or less revolutionary youth movements in the past and that are being used more frequently and more self-consciously in the latter half of the twentieth century. Since activist youth are facing established governments vastly superior in military power to their own, meeting them on equal terms, as in open battle, would be self-destructive. There remain two strategies suitable for the weak. The first attempts to disarm the opponent morally by a complete renunciation of force, subscribing to nonviolence, allowing helpless members to be imprisoned, tortured, or martyred, turning the other cheek, and exposing themselves to abuse by the powerful. This moral campaign of asserting one's injured rights aims at eroding the conscience of the powerful and enlisting public support. As a contemporary exponent of this strategy explains: "It is up to the citizenry, those outside power, to engage in permanent combat with the state, short of violent escalatory revolution, but beyond the gentility of the ballot box, to insure justice, freedom and well-being." This "permanent combat" is of course effective only against a liberal state.

The second method of overcoming the powerful is insurgent or guerrilla warfare. To an even greater extent than the first method it is accessible almost exclusively to the young, since guerrilla fighters must endure incredible deprivations and discomforts and a life of permanent danger. Regular governments, and especially

civilized governments, find it extremely difficult to cope with determined underground terrorism. For instance, General Grivas, of
Cyprus fame, explained in his book the practice of his execution
squads, whose task was to stalk their victims from the rear, shoot
them and make off, after passing the gun to a child or young girl
whom the British were not expected to charge with murder.

The two strategies may seem contradictory, and those who sub-
scribe to one usually reject the other with sincere horror; but when-
ever in history a revolt was directed against well-established adver-
saries, typical youth ideologies such as Anabaptism or anarchism
manifested themselves in irenic and belligerent shapes at the same
time, swinging easily and suddenly from one extreme to the other.
Both strategies reject legal methods of parliamentary procedures,
"electoral opium," compromise or slow progress. Both aim at the
overthrow and humiliation of the enemy; and both are supported
by the chiliastic hope that "the last shall be first."

The purpose and direction that young people find in movements
of rebellion helps many to overcome the insecurity and hopelessness
of a futile existence. The feeling of being able to cope with hardship and danger, the enjoyment of comradeship, and the acceptance
of their peers is basic to a sense of identity in the young. Even belonging to an antisocial and destructive movement can have a salu-
tary effect on the personality formation of a boy or girl, especially
in times of social dislocation.

One of the most serious consequences of "liberation movements"
is the inculcation of hostility in children. Basic political attitudes
and beliefs are formed in adolescence, and even earlier in life.
Prejudices learned in the first two decades of life are highly re-
sistant to later experience. The orgies of hatred now indulged in by
leaders of the young in various parts of the world greatly exceed
in scope and intensity the teaching of nationalism to children and
adults in the 150 years following the American and French revolutions. These hatreds will remain a long-lasting legacy of the age
of the "population explosion."

Social change is not engineered by youth, but it is most manifest
in youth. "The potential for change is concentrated in the cohorts
of young adults who are old enough to participate directly in the
movements impelled by change, but not old enough to have become
committed to an occupation, a residence, a family of procreation,

or a way of life." The direction of social change results from the total situation in which the young find themselves, including the types of leaders with whom they interact and the traditions and institutions they have inherited. The presence of a large contingent of young people in a population may make for a cumulative process of innovation and social and cultural growth; it may lead to elemental, directionless acting-out behavior; it may destroy old institutions and elevate new elites to power; and the unemployed energies of the young may be organized and directed by totalitarian rulers. The dynamism of its large and youthful populations distinguishes the crowded history of the twentieth century.

Anthony Esler

AFTER THE YOUTH REVOLUTION—WHAT?

Anthony Esler (b. 1934), professor of history at the College of William and Mary, has published two volumes of generational history: The Aspiring Mind of the Elizabethan Younger Generation *(1966) and* Bombs, Beards and Barricades: 150 Years of Youth in Revolt *(1972). His view of the Youth Revolution as a force for change is as positive as Feuer's is negative. In this article, Esler takes a single rebellious younger generation from the past as an illustrative example of the long-range influence of such revolts on the course of history.*

In recent years, a great deal of scholarly ingenuity has been lavished on the causes of that famous "revolt of the younger generation" that so bedeviled the world during the decade of the 1960s. Sociologists, psychologists, anthropologists, political scientists, and others have offered a wide variety of causal explanations for the youthful insurgency of the sixties. The debate over this startling intrusion of the youth into history has echoed well beyond the halls of

From Anthony Esler, "After the Youth Revolution—What? The French Generation of 1830 and Its Impact on History," read at the Southwestern Social Science Association, 1972.

academe as radicals, reactionaries, politicians, pundits, and others offered their varying answers to the disturbing question: Why did they do it? Why did so many young people rise up in revolt against their parents' world?

As the revolt of the frantic sixties fades into the past, however, an even more crucial question suggests itself to the historian. It is the question of consequences. Not Why did they rebel? but So what?

After the revolution is over and duly consigned to the newspaper morgues and the solemn pages of our histories—what have we got to show for it, after all? Did all that youthful marching and demonstrating, rioting, bombing, and dying for their causes make any difference in history?

For the historian with a special interest in the role of youth qua youth in modern times, furthermore, the question goes considerably beyond the interpretation of the 1960s. The prime claim of insurgent younger generations, past and present, has been that they represented a powerful *force* in history—that they would in fact change the world. "Our judgment has the weight of history itself," declared the leaders of the German *Burschenschaft* of 1815, the first of modern student movements—"it annihilates!" One hundred and fifty years later, the French students who occupied the Sorbonne in the spring of 1968 announced that they were going to destroy "not only the capitalist society but all industrial society . . . the consumer's society and the society of alienation. . . ." Their modest proposal: "We are creating a new and original world. Imagination is seizing power!"

The claims of the young rebels have often been extravagant and unrealistic. But the question still remains: If the youth revolts of the nineteenth and twentieth centuries have not brought in the millennium—have they made any difference at all? Or are they merely colorful episodes of no particular historical significance? Are they even counterproductive, as the conservative critic Lewis Feuer has claimed? Can we dismiss them, as he does, with the assertion that "the idealistic spirit" of the young militants "has done violence to itself and to others, and has been transmuted into a destructive force in human history"?

This is the question to which this essay addresses itself: not the causes, but the historic consequences—if any—of the typical modern youth revolt.

In order to maintain historical perspective, the prime case in point will not be the revolt of the American sixties, but rather an equally important youth revolution of the past—the famous "generation of 1830" in French history.

The French Revolution of July 1830 overthrew the last of the Bourbons and put Louis Philippe d'Orleans, the celebrated bourgeois king, on the throne of France. The revolution also triggered a major wave of social violence in that battered nation. Too many groups and classes of Frenchmen were dissatisfied with Louis Philippe and the bland constitutional monarchy he represented for the settlement of July to be accepted peacefully. For half a decade after those "three glorious days" in 1830, therefore, political and social discontent flared up repeatedly in Paris and the provinces. Assailed from left and right, the Orleanist monarchy seemed more than once to be trembling on the edge of dissolution during those tumultuous early years.

Traditional loyalties and class conflicts explain a good deal of this unrest. The pro-Bourbon peasant insurgency in the Vendée, for instance, was a case of ancient and profoundly conservative loyalties clashing with the new regime. Violent upheavals by artisans and proletarians, such as those which repeatedly turned the silk-weaving city of Lyon into a battleground, were matters of class interests in conflict. Much of the explosive ideological disaffection of the early 1830s, however, was generational in nature.

Certainly many of these rebellions struck contemporaries as essentially generational conflicts. Thus a Parisian, writing to a friend in the provinces in the immediate aftermath of the July revolution, declared that "Here the populace, the shopkeepers, even the workers are excellent; without the schoolboys [écoliers] everything would be perfectly calm." "The students are always ready to revolt," lamented a leading member of the Chamber of Deputies in 1831, "revolution against all constituted and recognized authority having become in their eyes 'the first of duties and the sweetest of pleasures!' " As we shall see, modern authorities have tended to confirm this contemporary impression. Too many of these militant republicans, Bonapartists, utopian Socialists, romantic Bohemians, and even Catholic reformers were young people—passionately, proudly, vociferously young—for this pervasive presence of the youth to be mere coincidence.

Frenchmen in the 1830s, like Americans in the 1960s, explained the youth rebellion in terms of purely current issues and present circumstance. They saw a younger generation overstimulated by the revolutionary rhetoric of 1830 rising in revolt against the bourgeois liberal establishment which the revolution of 1830 had brought to power. In the perspective of history, we have a not uncommon situation: a revolt of youthful radicals against a regime of middle-aged liberals.

But this matter merits a somewhat more complex analysis than this.

The French youth revolt of the years between 1830 and 1835 was not a monolithic entity—it took a number of forms. One theory of social generation has been developed by Karl Mannheim, the German sociologist.

In Mannheim's view, each of the ideologically-based subgroups mentioned above—republicans, Bonapartists, Socialists, and so on—would constitute a separate generation unit *within* the French generation of 1830. This concept, the generation unit, reflects the capacity of various subgroups within a given social generation to "work up" the common generational experience in "different specific ways." The present article will dwell on only three such units of the generation of 1830: the young republicans, the Saint-Simonian Socialists, and the romantic Bohemians.

The police spy Lucien de la Hodde described the republican leaders of the secret societies as "a generation of young men" among whom "July fell like a bomb. . . ." Authoritative modern scholarship tends to support this contemporary emphasis on the youth of the rebels of the earlier 1830s. John Plamenatz states categorically: "The Paris students were . . . the first organized republicans in nineteenth-century France" and characterizes the republican movement after 1830 in particular as "mostly young men tired of their elders. . . ."

The young republicans were certainly militant to a fault. For them, the constitutional monarchy of Louis Philippe was a totally unacceptable compromise. In their eyes, the highly touted liberalism of the "citizen king" fell far short of the real goal of the July revolution. That goal was nothing less than that ideal republic of reason and virtue Robespierre had dreamed of in the 1790s, revived now by a new generation of dreamers. In pursuit of this dream, revolutionary young men like Cavaignac, Barbès, and Auguste Blanqui took to the streets repeatedly in the years after 1830. They marched and demonstrated; they organized revolutionary secret societies; they raised the barricades once more.

The utopian Socialists of the thirties were also predominantly a youth movement. Literally "hundreds of young intellectuals" poured into the Saint-Simonian brotherhood alone in the 1830s, according to an exemplary study of one such convert. And an eye-witness described a typical Saint-Simonian meeting as an assemblage of youth, collected about their (typically older) gurus: "In the middle of a row of young men, two men of middle age [Enfantin and Bazard, the "fathers" of the movement] were the focus of all eyes."

The utopian dream of the Saint-Simonians was if anything more sweeping and exalted than that of the republicans, but it took far less aggressive and frightening forms. The comte de Saint-Simon was five years dead in 1830, but new generations had already begun to rally round his name and his vision of a technocratic Utopia guided and informed by an enlightened "New Christianity." In the 1830s, the religious and communal sides of the movement were clearly to the fore. Following the charismatic leadership of the hypnotic Prosper Enfantin in particular, surprising numbers of highly-educated young people attended the cult's emotional public meetings, donned its red, white, and blue uniforms, and moved into the Saint-Simonian communes, first in Paris and later on a farm at Ménilmontant, outside the city. There was a comical side to the doings of the Saint-Simonians, and they were lampooned in cartoons and musical reviews. But there was also something deeply disturbing to bourgeois Frenchmen about their communal life style, their strange songs and rituals, and the colorful rumors of sexual anarchy that clung to the growing movement.

The youth of the romantic Bohemians of the aptly named *Jeune-France* school of French letters, finally, was notorious. "I know some," a *Figaro* writer declared with tongue in cheek, "who went to read plays before the selection committee of the *Théâtre Française* in their nurses' arms. . . ." In a recent study of the origins of Bohemianism, Malcolm Easton describes the gaudily costumed left bank contingent who swarmed to the premiere of Victor Hugo's *Hernani* in 1830 as "young men of nineteen and twenty."

These romantically-inclined Bohemians represented an almost

antithetical way of "working up" the common generational experience from that of the militant young republicans. These art-for-art's-sake aesthetes, led by writers like long-haired Théophile Gautier, the bearded poet Gérard de Nerval, and the notorious "Wolfman" Borel, despised the bourgeois society of Louis Philippe's France as much as any of their generational contemporaries. Their response, however, was not to attack either the political or the economic bases of that society but, simply, to withdraw from it. Like the beatniks and hippies of a later day, the French Bohemians of the 1830s adopted a private language, life style, and ideological outlook all their own. Long-haired and bearded, dressed in outlandish costumes, they haunted the squalid streets of the left bank in search of wine, women, song—and beauty pure. "Withdrawn" though they were, however, these self-styled *bousingos* never lost an opportunity to ridicule, deceive, insult, or otherwise harass their top-hatted bourgeois elders. Their rebellion was every bit as real, in its countercultural way, as that of any other segment of their rebellious generation.

Through the tumultuous early 1830s, then, the youth revolution rolled on. From the Latin Quarter to the Louvre, the younger generation was in the streets, flaunting their wild panoply of long hair and gaudy costumes, radical ideologies and revolutionary rhetoric. Provincial cities also felt the erratic pressures of this youthful insurgency. And all this came against a background of incendiary discontent in the working-class ghettos, of rumored atheism and rampant immorality in the highest circles of society, of Satan worship, female emancipation, and other horrors too gruesome to dwell upon. Many contemporary observers feared that the very pillars of French civilization were crumbling around them.

It is perhaps a not unfamiliar picture.

But what came of it after all—of all that revolutionary sound and fury of the young?

The first consequence of the French youth revolution of the early 1830s was the repression of the middle and later thirties.

The liberal establishment put up with the young extremists for a surprisingly long time. The July monarchy was itself the product of a revolution, and its supporters were often sincerely dedicated to a more liberal order than that of the autocratic Bourbons. From the "citizen king" to the neighborhood greengrocer, bourgeois Frenchmen sang the *Marseillaise* and hailed the tricolor flag almost as enthusiastically as the young republicans themselves. Much of the press was scathingly opposed to Louis Philippe, and proceeded to give the dashing young rebels a strongly positive public image. During the early 1830s, liberal judges and liberal juries often refused to convict young people charged with riot and conspiracy. Even such a full-time revolutionary as Auguste Blanqui had to preach sedition in the courtroom itself before he could be bundled off to serve a short prison term.

But several years of such arrogant challenges to the status quo—in the press, in the courts, and in the streets—finally triggered the inevitable reaction.

Of the three subgroups of this rebellious young generation mentioned, the Saint-Simonians were the first to go down. In 1832, Prosper Enfantin and other leaders of the Ménilmontant commune outside Paris were hustled into court as an offense to public morality. Despite a ringing courtroom assault on "the system" by the bearded Enfantin, the commune was ordered to disband, its leaders sentenced to a year in prison. The group, already deeply in debt and fragmented by personal and ideological feuds, scarcely survived these blows. In 1834, only a handful of the faithful set out for the mystic East on the brotherhood's last quixotic quest—the search for the woman messiah.

The turn of the revolutionary republicans came in 1834 and 1835, when a repressive new Law on Associations and the so-called Monster Trial of 164 radical leaders wiped out their most formidable secret society. By that time, the liberal bourgeoisie had come to see Cavaignac and Blanqui and their ilk, not as the dashing heroes of the July revolution, or even as misguided young idealists, but as dangerous subversives. The government was thus finally able to convince the public of the allegedly close ties between the youthful revolutionary dreamers and such bloody revolutionary realities as the 1834 workingmen's uprisings in Lyon, Paris, and other cities. Blanqui and Barbès were soon in prison, Cavaignac fled into exile, the Republican societies and publications suppressed, the movement broken.

The romantic Bohemians, by contrast, were never really killed off at all: they just seemed to fade away. The public turned icily away from their artistic extravagances, their amoral life styles, their dissident values. Despised, and worse yet, ignored, the *bousingos* began to see themselves as the archetypal artist-rejected-by-society, the Chatterton of Alfred de Vigny's play. Many gave up their artistic vocations altogether and drifted out of Bohemia, home to the provinces, or perhaps into some cozy niche in the bureaucracy. Théophile Gautier sank so low as to take a job with the newspapers. Gérard de Nerval had a nervous breakdown. "Wolfman" Borel fled into a miserable self-imposed exile, first in Champagne, subsequently in North Africa.

By the later 1830s, then, a miasma of gloom and disarray, a deepening conviction of failure, had settled down over the dissenting youth. Maxine du Camp recalled it as "a general weakening of the spirit which made the heart heavy and sad, which darkened thought and made death welcome as a deliverance. The generation [of the late 1830s] had a youth of despairing sadness. . . ." By 1840, Louis Blanc was cursing the "silent generation" that had succeeded the hell-raisers of the early thirties: "This silence is fatal," he lamented, "this quiet is sinister. Our calm is that of exhaustion . . . the enervation of souls and the abasement of character."

In the short run, then, the only visible consequence of the great youth revolution seemed to be repression for the rebels and defeat for their causes. Louis Philippe, the "king of the greengrocers," went on his unmajestic way. Auguste Blanqui vanished into the dungeons of Mont-Saint-Michel, the Saint-Simonians into Hither Asia. The left bank Bohemians cut their hair and became hat salesmen.

But was there no more to it than that?

Seen from the vantage point of 150 years of history, the revolt of the French generation of 1830 actually takes on a great deal more significance than those who survived the debacle of the mid-thirties would have believed. Each of the "generation units" dealt with here made important contributions to the shaping of things to come.

There is no question of the importance of the republican contribution to French history. In 1829, forty years after the great French Revolution of 1789, the very word "republican" was proscribed, along with such subversive symbols of that discredited social experiment as the tricolor and the *Marseillaise*. The young ideologues of the 1830s were the first to summon the courage to put the old ideals of 1789 and 1793 back into print once more—to declare openly, *"Je suis républicain!"* The fury of their dedication to this vanished political ideal thrust it so rudely back into the realm of public discourse that no amount of repression could drive it once more into oblivion. Republicanism was a living alternative in French politics from that time on. More, it was the wave of the future. All that followed, from the French republics of 1848 and 1871 through the fourth and fifth republics of our own century, may be seen to stem from that great recovery of a defeated dream.

The utopian Socialists—of which the Saint-Simonians were not the least important branch—also left their mark on French history, and on the history of Europe at large. The very word *socialisme* first came into common use in France during the 1830s, thanks to the writing, speaking, and organizing of the youthful followers of Saint-Simon, Fourier, Étienne Cabet, and others. Celebrated prophets of the new gospel like Louis Blanc and Proudhon were shaped during their youth in the thirties. During the 1840s, these men in turn helped to structure the socialistic thinking of one even more important to the growing movement than they—the young German exile Karl Marx.

Given the brutal realities of the early Industrial Revolution, socialism was perhaps an ideal whose time was bound to come, sooner or later. Nevertheless, it was the young dissenters of the generation of 1830 who had the nerve to espouse the ideas of isolated, dying prophets like Saint-Simon and Fourier, and turn those eccentric ideas into the ideological backbone of a crusading movement for social justice.

The romantic outcasts of the Latin Quarter, finally, created by sheer inadvertence one of the characteristic social institutions of modern times: the Bohemian counterculture. Their literary and artistic contributions, while far from contemptible, cannot match those of their mentors, the first romantic generation in France—Victor Hugo, Dumas *père,* Balzac, George Sand, et al. But these second-generation romantics of the 1830s did forge a new life style, a culture all their own, separate from and militantly opposed to the morals and mores of the society in which they lived. This left bank subculture of the 1830s, led by young men like Théophile Gautier and "Wolfman" Borel, was "the first Bohemia," the first of modern countercultures.

As the bourgeois way of life has spread from class to class and continent to continent, the Bohemian too has thrived. Over the past century and a half, Bohemian "liberated zones" have spread every-where—from Murget's Paris of the 1840s to the *fin de siècle* version of Gaughin and Toulouse-Lautrec; from London's Soho to New York's Greenwich Village; from the North Beach of the beatniks to the Haight-Ashbury of the hippies. The ideologies may differ—though there are certain remarkable continuities—but the essential life style, the antibourgeois Bohemian subculture itself, has remained as a lasting memorial to the revolt of the French generation of 1830.

In essence, this pattern of short-run defeat and long-range victory is not limited to the French generation of 1830. Rather the youth re-volt constitutes a crucial *middle term* in the process of social change.

Rebellious younger generations themselves seldom *create* many radically new ideas of their own. They are even more seldom suc-cessful in *imposing* their revolutionary notions on society at large. What they *do* do—and do surprisingly well—is take up the wild ideas of unhonored prophets and pass them on to the pragmatic politicians who *can* turn ideas into social institutions.

The process is thus two-fold.

Stage one begins when the young ideologues, far less committed to the status quo than their more solidly socialized elders, advo-cate unconventional ideas, some of which may have much greater long-range social utility than their elders are capable of seeing. Thus the French youth of 1830 took up the discredited dream of a revolutionary republic, the unreasonable vision of a technocratic utopia, and the most extravagant fustian spun out by Victor Hugo and his fellow artistic wildmen of the 1820s.

Stage two of this generational contribution to social change boils down to a monstrous and extremely effective propaganda campaign. The young crusaders themselves dream of transforming society in their own time, through their own vehement, sometimes violent efforts. Typically, this does not take place. But those efforts do burn some awareness of new problems, or new solutions, into the public consciousness. Years of marching, demonstrating, rioting, and fight-ing in the streets make *socialisme* a truism of French social thought, or make it possible once more to say in public: *Je suis républicain!* Nothing may come of it today—or tomorrow. But if the idea has validity and social value, it will live and bear institutional fruit in its own good time.

In conclusion, the young rebels *make* the world listen to its most unhonored prophets. When enough people are listening, the pragmatic politicians surely will be found to turn the dreams of isolated social thinkers into the realities that govern millions. As a crucial *first constituency* for radical ideas, as a middle term between the unknown or rejected ideologue and the manipulator of political power, youth revolutions play an essential part in the dynamics of modern social change.

Suggestions for Additional Reading

Much of the seminal theoretical work on the generational factor in history has been done in continental Europe, particularly in Germany, Spain, and France. An increasing amount of this theoretical material, however, has been translated into English in recent years. American social scientists in particular have also begun to take a larger interest in the generational approach, especially since the youth revolts of the 1960s.

Two of the most important seminal discussions of the generation in history are those by Ortega and Mannheim excerpted in this book. For the complete English versions of these crucial articles, see the chapters on the subject in José Ortega y Gasset, *The Modern Theme,* translated by James Cleugh (London, 1931); *Man and Crisis,* translated by Mildred Adam (New York, 1958); and Karl Mannheim's two-part essay, "The Problem of Generations," *Essays on the Sociology of Knowledge,* edited by Paul Kecskemeti (New York, 1952). Ortega's disciple Julián Marís presents a rather more systematic account of the Spanish philosopher's ideas on the subject in *Generations: A Historical Method,* translated by Harold G. Raley (University, Alabama, 1970). Mannheim's theoretical approach is elaborated by Marvin Rintala, excerpted in this book and in "A Generation in Politics," cited below.

Works by historians, political scientists, sociologists, anthropologists, psychologists, and others concerned with youth movements have become increasingly numerous in recent years. These works have developed such illuminating generationally-related concepts as the political generation, the birth cohort, political socialization, and the youthful identity crisis.

See, among other works in this category: Alan B. Spitzer's comprehensive article, "The Historical Problem of Generations," *American Historical Review* 78 (1973):1353–1985; Herbert Butterfield, *The Discontinuities Between the Generations in History* (Cambridge, 1972); Robert L. Tyler, "Of Generations, Generation Gaps, and History," *Connecticut Review* 5 (1971):5–12; Marvin Rintala, "A Generation in Politics," *Review of Politics* 25 (1963):509–522; Robert E. Lane, "Fathers and Sons: Foundations of Political Belief," *American Sociological Review* 24 (1959):502–511; Norman B. Ryder, "The Cohort as a Concept in the Study of Social Change," *American*

Sociological Review 30 (1965):843–861; Shmuel N. Eisenstadt, *From Generation to Generation: Age Groups and Social Structure* (Glencoe, Illinois, 1956); Konrad Lorenz, "The Enmity Between Generations and Its Probable Causes," *Psychoanalytic Review* 57 (1970): 334–404; Erik H. Erikson, *Childhood and Society,* 2nd ed. (New York, 1963); and Kenneth Keniston, "Youth: A 'New' Stage of Life," *American Scholar* 39 (1970):631–654.

Students with the appropriate language skills are urged to look at some of the still untranslated generational theory from Europe, including: Pedro Laín Entralgo, *Las géneraciones en la historia* (Madrid, 1945); Eduard Wechssler, *Die Generation als Jugendreihe und Ihr Kampf um die Denkform* (Leipzig, 1930); François Mentré, *Les générations sociales* (Paris, 1920); and Yves Renouard, "La notion de génération en histoire," *Revue historique* 260 (1953):1–23.

Two historical surveys of the youth revolution of the past century and a half reveal a strongly generational bent: Lewis S. Feuer, *The Conflict of Generations: The Character and Significance of Student Movements* (New York, 1969), and Anthony Esler, *Bombs, Beards, and Barricades: 150 Years of Youth in Revolt* (New York, 1972). See also two unpublished dissertations, available on University Microfilms: B. J. Verbal, *Youth Movements in Modern European History, 1815–1914* (Carnegie-Mellon University, 1971), and Eric Josephson, *Political Youth Organizations in Europe, 1900–1950* (Columbia University, 1960). On the most recent wave of the youth revolution, which crested in 1968, see: Stephen Spender, *The Year of the Young Rebels* (New York, 1969); Joseph A. Califano, *The Student Revolution: A Global Confrontation* (New York, 1970); and George Paloczi-Horvath, *Youth Up in Arms: A Political and Social Survey 1955–1970* (London, 1971); as well as Barbara and John Ehrenreich, *Long March, Short Spring* (New York, 1969).

There is considerable literature on youthful dissent in each of the major European states during the nineteenth and twentieth centuries. Many of these accounts are essentially generational, emphasizing the role of historical and social factors in shaping each generation of young revolutionaries. The following selections generally are representative of this tendency.

On the German Student Unions, among the most useful sources available in English are Gunther Eyck, "The Political Theories and Activities of the German Academic Youth between 1815 and 1819,"

The Journal of Modern History 27 (1955):27–38, and George W. Spindler, *The Life of Karl Follen* (Chicago, 1917), the latter focusing on the most celebrated leader of the extremist wing of the *Burschenschaften.* On the Student Unions after the Karlsbad Decrees, consult Rolland Ray Lutz, "The German Revolutionary Student Movement, 1819–1833," *Central European History* 4 (1971):215–241; Douglas Hales, "The Persecution of the Demagogues in Germany, 1833–1842," read at the Southwestern Social Science Association in 1972; and the chapter on the demagogues in Leonard Krieger, *The German Idea of Freedom: History of a Political Tradition* (Boston, 1957).

On German youth movements from the late nineteenth century through the Hitler Youth, Walter Z. Laqueur, *Young Germany: A History of the German Youth Movement* (New York, 1962) provides the best overall coverage. In addition, see H. Becker's evocative *German Youth, Bond or Free* (New York, 1946). On youth in politics during the period of Hitler's rise to power, see Wolfgang Zorn, "Student Politics in the Weimar Republic," *Journal of Contemporary History* 5 (1970): 128–143, and the widely cited contemporary journalistic account by Alice Hamilton of the *New York Times,* "The Youth Who Are Hitler's Strength," reprinted in John Weiss, ed., *Nazis and Fascists in Europe, 1918–1945* (Chicago, 1969). See also Sigmund Neumann's brief generational analysis of the Nazi leadership in his *The Future in Perspective* (New York, 1946), pp. 221–225. For the Hitler Youth itself, there are, besides Laqueur, such specialized studies as Lawrence D. Walker, *Hitler Youth and Catholic Youth, 1933–1936* (Washington, 1970) and such wartime productions as Gregor A. Zimmer, *Education for Death: The Making of the Nazi* (London, 1941).

Comparatively recent accounts of Mazzini as ideologue and organizer of youthful secret societies include E. E. Y. Hales' balanced study of *Mazzini and the Secret Societies: The Making of a Myth* (New York, 1956); Stringfellow Barr, *Mazzini, Portrait of an Exile* (New York, 1934); and G. O. Griffith's strongly pro-Mazzini analysis, *Mazzini: Prophet of Modern Europe* (London, 1932). On Young Italy in particular, the English-speaking student is reduced to the old study by Alexander Baillie Cochrane, *Young Italy* (London, 1850). For the Italian revolutionary underground in general, however, consult such studies as George Macauley Trevelyan, *Daniel Manin and the Venetian Revolution of 1848* (London and New York, 1907) and M. C. Wicks, *The Italian Exiles in London, 1816–1848* (Manchester, 1937).

On twentieth-century youth movements in Italy, particularly on Mussolini's pioneering efforts to channel youthful energies into the service of the totalitarian state, see Renato Marzolo, *The Youth Movement in Italy* (Rome, 1939); Domenico S. Piccoli, *The Youth Movement in Italy* (Rome, 1936); and Michael A. Ledden, "Italian Fascism and Youth," *The Journal of Contemporary History* 4 (1969): 137–154.

The best single book on the revolution of 1848 in the Austrian capital is R. John Rath, *The Viennese Revolution of 1848* (Austin, Texas, 1957). See also a scholarly work of piety for an ancestor, Josephine Goldmark, *Pilgrims of '48: One Man's Part in the Austrian Revolution of 1848* (New Haven, 1930); Arnold Whitridge, *Men in Crisis: The Revolution of 1848* (New York, 1967); William J. McGrath, "Student Radicalism in Vienna," *Journal of Contemporary History* 2 (1967):183–201; and the relevant chapter in Priscilla Robertson, *Revolutions of 1848: A Social History* (Princeton, 1952).

Two contemporary accounts which vividly recreate the revolutionary year in Vienna and the crucial role of the Academic Legion are: William H. Stiles, *Austria in 1848 and 1849,* 2 vols. (New York, 1852), perhaps the best contemporary study; and Berthold Auerbach, *Narrative of Events in Vienna from Latour to Windischgrätz,* translated by John Edward Taylor (London, 1849), a day-by-day account focused on the city itself.

A vast amount of historical scholarship has been devoted to the predominantly youthful revolutionary movements of nineteenth- and twentieth-century Russia. Probably the best overall survey is Avrahm Yarmolinsky, *Road to Revolution: A Century of Russian Radicalism* (New York, 1956). A good part of the nineteenth century is also covered, in more depth, in Franco Venturi, *Roots of Revolution: A History of the Populist and Socialist Movements in Nineteenth-Century Russia,* translated by Francis Haskell (London, 1960).

On the youthful secret societies and radical study groups of the earlier nineteenth century, see: A. G. Mazour, *The First Russian Revolution, 1825* (Berkeley, 1937); Marc Raeff, *The Decembrist Movement* (New York, 1966); and Isaiah Berlin, "A Marvelous Decade 1838–48: The Birth of the Russian Intelligentsia," in Sidney Harcave, ed., *Readings in Russian History* (New York, 1962).

On the pivotal midcentury generations, consult Franco Venturi's thorough study cited above, *Roots of Revolution*; E. Lampert's two books, *Sons against Fathers* (Oxford, 1965) and *Studies in Rebellion* (London, 1960); Ronald Hingley, *Nihilists: Russian Radicals and Revolutionaries in the Reign of Alexander II (1855–81)* (London, 1967); and Ronald Seth, *The Russian Terrorists: The Story of the Narodniki* (London, 1966). Revealing biographical studies include James H. Billington, *Mikhailovsky and Russian Populism* (Oxford, 1958); David Footman, *Red Prelude: The Life of the Russian Terrorist Zhelyabov* (New Haven, 1945); and such autobiographies as Peter Kropotkin's *Memoirs of a Revolutionist* (London, 1931) and Catherine Breshkovsky, *Hidden Springs of the Russian Revolution: Personal Memoirs of Katerina Breshkovskaia,* edited by Lincoln Hutchinson (Stanford, 1931).

For insights into the generation of Lenin in the decades before World War I, see Bertram D. Wolfe's stimulating study of the early years of the underground Marxists, *Three Who Made a Revolution* (Boston, 1948). See also N. K. Krupskaya's volume of *Reminiscences of Lenin,* translated by Bernard Isaacs (Moscow, 1959). On the *Komsomol* of Soviet Russia, see Ralph T. Fisher, Jr., *Pattern for Soviet Youth* (New York, 1959).

The Hungarian revolt spawned a large number of personal memoirs of the street fighting, as well as some serious efforts to analyze the insurrection more deeply. Among the latter are Paul Kecskemeti, *The Unexpected Revolution: Social Forces in the Hungarian Uprising* (Palo Alto, California, 1969) and Francis S. Wagner, ed., *The Hungarian Revolution in Perspective* (Washington, 1967). Eyewitness accounts, mostly by young participants, include Noel Barber, *A Handful of Ashes: A Personal Testament of the Battle of Budapest* (London, 1957) and Andor Heller, *No More Comrades* (Chicago, 1957), as well as the two memoirs excerpted in this book.

Some studies on earlier youthful factions and youth movements in the Balkans and Turkey are: Communist Youth Union of Hungary, *Hungarian Youth Movement 1919–1957* (Budapest, 1957); E. E. Ramsaur, *The Young Turks: Prelude to the Revolution of 1908* (Princeton, 1957); Vladimir Didijer, *The Road to Sarajevo* (New York, 1966); and the appropriate chapters of Robert Kann, *The Habsburg Empire* (New York, 1957) on the Young Czechs.

There are many books about the May Days of 1968 in Paris. Among the works available in English are Raymond Aron's less than enthusiastic *The Elusive Revolution: Anatomy of a Student Revolt,* translated by Gordon Clough (New York, 1969); Alain Touraine, *The May Movement . . . Birth of a Social Movement,* translated by Leonard F. X. Mayhew (New York, 1971); Belden A. Fields' precisely focused *Student Politics in France: A Study of the Union Nationale des Étudiants de France* (New York, 1970); and Patrick Seale and Maureen McConville, *Red Flag/Black Flag: French Revolution 1968* (New York, 1968).

Hervé Bourges' collection of interviews, *The French Student Revolt: The Leaders Speak,* translated by B. R. Brewster (New York, 1968) is valuable as a source of participant attitudes, as are such expressions of rank-and-file sentiment as the massive collection of documents by Alain Schnapp and Pierre Vidal-Naquet, *The French Student Uprising, November 1967–June 1968,* translated by Maria Jolas (Boston, 1971) and the "Atelier Populaire's" anthology of *Posters from the Revolution* (London, 1969). The photographs which fill Gilbert Kahn's *Paris a brulé* (Paris, 1968) are among the most powerful evocations of "moving in the streets" available anywhere.

The best study of nineteenth-century French revolutionary movements is John Plamenatz, *The Revolutionary Movement in France 1815–1871* (London, 1952), which takes due note of the youth of many of the participants. Two detailed studies of early nineteenth-century youth revolts are Alan B. Spitzer's *Old Hatreds and Young Hopes: The French Carbonari Against the Bourbon Restoration* (Cambridge, Massachusetts, 1971) and Anthony Esler's article on "Youth in Revolt: The French Generation of 1830," in Robert Bezucha, *Essays in Modern Social History* (New York, 1972). An interesting contemporary account of young French revolutionaries of the first half of the nineteenth century as seen by a police spy in their ranks is Lucien de la Hodde, *History of Secret Societies and of the Republican Party of France from 1830 to 1848* (Philadelphia, 1856).

John Eros's "The Positivist Generation of French Republicanism," *Sociological Review,* new series, 3 (1955):255–277, provides a convincing generational approach to the development of a political ideology in the second half of the nineteenth century. Phyllis H. Stock, "Students versus the University in Pre-World War Paris," *French Historical Studies* 7 (1971):93–110, is a more orthodox historical examination of twentieth-century youth movements.

On the comparatively mild ferment of age-related social dissent in the British Isles during the nineteenth and twentieth centuries, see the interesting psychohistorical article by Howard Wolf, "British Fathers and Sons, 1773–1913," *Psychoanalytic Review* 52 (1965): 197–213; Paul Wilkinson's more orthodox "English Youth Movements, 1908–30," *The Journal of Contemporary History* 4 (1969):3–23; and Margaret McCarthy's memoir, *Generation in Revolt* (London, 1953).

On the political faction known as Young England, see B. R. Jerman, *The Young Disraeli* (Princeton, 1960). On the role of youth in the perennial Irish problem, consult Charles Gavan Duffy, *Young Ireland,* rev. ed. (London, 1896) and R. Dudley Edwards, "The Contribution of Young Ireland to the Development of the Irish National Idea," in Seamus Pender, ed., *Feilscribhinn Torna: Essays and Studies Presented to Professor Taghg Ua Donnchadha* (Cork, 1947).